LITERATURE AND FILM
IN THE HISTORICAL DIMENSION

UMETLD

LITERATURE AND FILM
IN THE HISTORICAL DIMENSION

Selected Papers from the Fifteenth Annual
Florida State University
Conference on Literature and Film

Edited by John D. Simons

UNIVERSITY PRESS OF FLORIDA
GAINESVILLE

Library of Congress Cataloging-in-Publication Data

Florida State University Conference on Literature and Film (15th : 1990)
     Literature and film in the historical dimension : selected papers from the
Fifteenth Annual Florida State University Conference on Literature and Film
/ edited by John D. Simons.
       p.   cm.
     Includes bibliographical references and index.
     ISBN 0-8130-1285-6 (alk. paper)
     1. Literature and history—Congresses.   2. History in literature—
Congresses.   3. Motion pictures and history—Congresses.   4. Historical
films—History and criticism—Congresses.   I. Simons, John D.   II. Title.
PN50.F57   1990
791.43'658—dc20
                                                                                93-35012
                                                                                CIP

The University Press of Florida is the scholarly publishing agency for the State
University System of Florida, comprised of Florida A & M University, Florida
Atlantic University, Florida International University, Florida State University,
University of Central Florida, University of Florida, University of North Florida,
University of South Florida, and University of West Florida.

University Press of Florida
15 Northwest 15th Street
Gainesville, FL 32611

CONTENTS

1. INTRODUCTION: STORYTELLING AS A COGNITIVE INSTRUMENT

John D. Simons

THIS COLLECTION OF ESSAYS CONTAINS selected papers from the Fifteenth Annual Conference on Literature and Film held at Florida State University in the winter of 1990. The theme of the conference, "Literature and Film in the Historical Dimension," invited the participants to explore the relation between aspects of history, literature, and film. The authors employ a diversity of methodologies as they probe the many ways literary and cinematic works strive to make sense of the world—past and present, public and private.

What first strikes us about the relation between artistic and historical narrative is the difference in objectives. Aristotle was the first to comment on this subject. In his *Poetics* he observes that since poetry deals with "universals" and history with "particulars," poetry expresses a higher truth. Although Aristotle ranks history lower than poetry, we shall see that perhaps the two have more in common than not.

Traditionally, historians aim at reconstructing an accurate record of the past. They make specific statements about certain events and are judged by how well their statements correspond to the tracts. Still, they enjoy a good deal of freedom in the selection of the tracts and in evaluating the relationship between them. Striving for objectivity, they guard against being influenced by ideological preconceptions, such as Marxism or social Darwinism, or by the exigencies of their own personalities. Although these factors cannot be entirely eliminated, they can be minimized. This approach is alien to those working in literature and film because artists approach their material subjectively. Their aim is not historical truth but the fictionalization of truth with the purpose of illuminating the human condition.

Although history and the creative arts have different objectives, they achieve their goals in a similar way. When the historian's compilation of facts and sources gets to a certain point, sense must be made of it. Intelligibility is achieved by treating the historical events as components of a story. Storytelling is a cognitive instrument for making events understandable. Historical accounts owe part of their explanatory success to the development of a coherent narrative out of raw material by a process called emplotment, which the historian Hayden White defines as "the encodation of the facts contained in the chronicle as components of specific kinds of plot-structure. . . ."[1] The author decides what is to be emphasized, subordinated, or left out—how to characterize and how to describe. Since historical events are neutral in value, a point of view must be chosen.[2] These are the same techniques employed in creative writing or in filmmaking. For example, the way any given account of the American Civil War is emplotted depends on the point of view. Some view the war as a tragedy, while others romanticize it; it appeared one way to the abolitionists, another way to the Southern landowners. Here literature and history are closest. Extrapolating from Aristotle's definition, in the *Poetics*, of tragedy as an imitation of action, Northrop Frye defines historical writing as "a verbal imitation of action, or events put into the form of words" (*FI* 53). Like the historian the creative writer also uses words to imitate actions, with the difference that the writer seldom claims to make any statements of fact. Human actions are imitated "because they are typical and recurring"— rituals, in other words (*FI* 53). To imitate ritual is myth, says Frye.

What Aristotle calls mythos is equivalent to the English word myth. Hence, at some point the historian's scheme "becomes mythical in shape, and so approaches the poetic in structure" (*FI* 53). Claude Levi-Strauss holds a similar view: "In spite of worthy . . . attempts to become different, history, as its clear-sighted practitioners are obliged to admit, can never completely divest itself of myth."[4] Even so, Frye remarks on the likelihood that "to tell a historian that what gives shape to his book is a myth would sound to him vaguely insulting" (*FI* 55).

Writing on the relation between literature and history, White observes the general reluctance of scholars in his field to regard historical narratives for what they are, ". . . verbal fictions the contents of which are as much invented as found, and the forms of which have more in common with their counterparts in literature than they have with those in the sciences" (HT 42). In other words the form, which the historian imposes on the facts, is an artifice, a product of the imagination. Levi-Strauss goes farthest in deflating claims of strict scientific objectivity in historical writing. He says that when it comes to putting the facts into story form, the writer gains coherence by making the facts fit the story form. "In a system of this type, alleged historical continuity is secured only by dint of fraudulent outlines."[5]

In any case, the essential goal of mimesis is instruction and clarification. In literature and film it illuminates human action; in history it clarifies the disparate particulars of something that happened in the past. The result in each case is that we undergo a learning experience identified by Aristotle as the highest human pleasure.

The impossibility of writing history impartially and objectively informs T. O'Neill's study of Vincenzo Consolo's *Il sorriso dell'ignoto mariaio*. Like many other writers Consolo is concerned with what happens to the past when it is subjected to linguistic expression and filtered through the teller's value system and cultural heritage. The account, of course, can be colored in many ways. O'Neill demonstrates this by clarifying and examining the three types of narrative. The author focuses primarily on the appendices, which are later reconstructions of the

3

events recounted. A scholarly account of the 1856 uprising in Cefalù written in 1904 in dry, lifeless prose contrasts with and earlier idealistic, romantic account of Garibaldi's landing. In the final analysis the protagonist Mondralissa observes "the impossibility of writing if one does not wish to betray, to create fraud, and at the same time the necessity and the compulsion to do it." Not only did Garibaldi defeat his adversaries in Sicily, he also unwittingly destroyed the country's language and culture. This explains "his and our failure to write the real history of the Risorgimento in Sicily in its own language."

A good example of what happens when the facts are made to fit preconceptions is provided by Judy Gibert in her analysis of the seven part television series "The Voyage of Charles Darwin." The only historian contributing to this selection, Gibert compares the historical record of Darwin and Victorian England with the image created in the series and finds that the two do not coincide. The series depicts Darwin as a loner, a maverick, and a misfit with little formal education—a false picture. In fact, he was a member of an active scientific community. The documentary fails to show how his ideas emerged from his readings and association with other scientists; rather, it emphasizes his idea of natural selection as a lone man's "accidental inspiration." Still more invidious is the conception of the nature of science and its public role. Scientists, Gibert points out, are presented as nonconformists on the fringe of society. The series wrongly portrays scientific discovery as the result of inspiration or chance. In fact, science is a gradual process involving many people and the synthesis of many ideas—not a realm outside the community in opposition to traditional values. In short, the series illustrates what happens when historical facts are filtered through someone's ideological preconceptions. Perhaps misconceptions would be a better term.

The problem of falsifying history is also the subject of Victoria Carchidi's article. Her analysis of the films *Cry Freedom* and *Dry White Season,* and the novels on which they are based, illuminates the difficulties and pitfalls awaiting any director who tries to bring historical or contemporary events to the screen. If directors agree with Aristotle's contention in the *Poetics* that art is not in the service of history, and instead tells things as they might have or could have been, then they are free to invent a story that gives an overall picture. Loosely basing their stories on history, they are at liberty to rearrange the incidents, to invent characters and situations. All this is permissible if they capture the spirit of the time. The directors of these two films, Carchidi says, have succumbed to the temptation to present the problems of apartheid through the eyes of the Anglo-Saxon middle class. Carchidi's point is that in telling the story of the black reformer Steve Biko according to white patterns of thinking, the directors have given a false picture of the circumstances and so capture neither the true nature of Biko's thought nor the real situation in South Africa.

The problem of creative freedom versus historical accuracy is addressed once again by Elaine McAllister in her "Film as Historical Text: *Danton*." In adapting the Polish play *Danton* for filming, screenwriter Jean-Claude Carriere grossly distorted well-known historical facts and created fictitious situations with the object of making Robespierre the villain of the French Revolution and Danton its hero. Both scholars and film critics excoriated the director and the screenwriter for willful distortion. The French were particularly incensed because they have always regarded Robespierre as the true hero of the Revolution. Carriere and Wadja defended themselves in ways similar to Aristotle, claiming that it is not the business of the artist to record facts. Facts in themselves are value neutral. They convey no message immutable for all time. They mean different things to different societies and to different ages. It is the artist's job to discern and convey message and meaning, not to cater to popular sentiment. Still, the controversy surrounding the film indicates that if directors diverge too far from traditional viewpoints their work will gain acceptance only with difficulty.

The next group of essays focuses on the role of social forces in determining a community's outlook and behavior. Majda Anderson examines the novel *Dangerous Liaisons* and its film adaptation within the

5

historical context of the struggle for power, and she arrives at a fresh interpretation. As a feminist, Anderson finds Michel Foucault's ideas about the close relation between sex, power, and pleasure particularly relevant. Employing his ideas, she shows how the novel and the film follow a traditional pattern common to human behavior. According to Foucault, the greatest sustainable pleasure is power over others. It can be exerted in many ways. In the everyday world it is usually achieved through positive or negative reinforcement, but the most subtle kind is found in the relation between knowledge and confession, such as reflected in *Dangerous Liaisons*. Here power is acquired through knowledge, which in turn is obtained through "discourse" with others. Valmont and de Marteuil gain information from Cecile, de Tourvel, the servants, and from intercepted letters they use to manipulate others. To the manipulator it matters little whether the victim is aware of the situation. Cecile, her mother, and Danceny do not know they are part of an intrigue; de Tourvel is ignorant of Valmont's maneuvering, and he, in turn, does not know that de Marteuil is orchestrating the whole show. Where Valmont pursues his quarry purely for the pleasure involved, de Merteuil's gratification resides in dominating men to "avenge her sex"; she bitterly resents that women have always been subservient to men. Anderson argues that De Marteuil is finally destroyed because she gains too much power: "The inherent prejudice prevalent in the patriarchal society against women acquiring too much power revels in the downfall of those who attempt to overstep the undeclared boundaries."

Although Nancy Lane does not bring Foucault's ideas to bear in her piece on *Hiroshima mon amour*, his remarks about the benefits of discourse are quite relevant. Foucault observes that confession becomes a ritual "in which the expression alone, independently of its external consequences produces intrinsic modifications in the person who articulates it; it exonerates, redeems, and purifies him, it unburdens him of his wrongs; liberates him, and promises him salvation."[6] Similarly, the French woman in the film has been unable to come to terms with the death of her German lover and her subsequent imprisonment in the cellar. It is only when she narrates the episode to her Japanese lover many years later that she finally gains understanding. In so doing her past love and suffering are exorcised, allowing her to recover the voice and body she had lost at Nevers. The self-knowledge she acquires through confession culminates in the freedom of self-determination.

Lane arrives at similar conclusions by approaching the film from Marguerite Duras's conception of public and private history, storytelling, and understanding. Accordingly, the woman realizes that there is something fixed in her past that is retrievable but unintelligible so far. It became intelligible only after "it was emplotted and narrated." Putting her life into story form allows her to free herself from the past and to "reintegrate herself as seen and seer."

Lane's other objective is to examine the evolution of Duras's conception of the past. As an example of her early work, the film follows traditional narrative conventions. It regards storytelling as selecting, arranging, and ordering things that happened in order to make sense of them. Lane draws attention to instances in the film that foreshadow Duras's later experimental style in which she questions even the concept of *histoire,* public or private, and is convinced that in the end it is "not tellable." This is clear from the decentralizing effect of the camera and the voice-over, which work to disperse the narrative unity.

Storytelling as a way to impart meaning to one's existence also figures in Mark Hedborn's study of Brautigan's *Dreaming of Babylon.* He employ's Lacanian psychology and certain principles of postmodernism to resolve the structure of the novel and protagonist C. Card's enigmatic behavior. Card creates a fantasy world located in ancient Babylon, in which he stars as the hero in a series of detective adventures. He spends so much time daydreaming that it impairs his ability to function in the real world. In deciphering the cause of Card's schizophrenic behavior, Hedborn suggests that Card is struggling to create a stable seat of personal identity. The lack of a stable identity generates the storytelling process. Thus, the novel is also about how Brautigan

7

composes. Card selects his titles, plots, and characters from comic strips, films, and books, which he then cobbles together into story form. It could be mentioned that the novelist Thomas Mann admitted to composing in a similar way, although he strove for narrative consistency. Brautigan as a postmodernist is, of course, indifferent to linear continuity. He splices genres and attitudes; he relishes the blurring of fantasy and reality, moods, and cultural levels. He neither affirms nor criticizes but presents the world blankly, dissolving literature into parody and irony.

Rita di Giuseppe's study of Edith Wharton's *House of Mirth* examines how people fall victims to social forces they do not understand. Printed in 1905, Wharton's novel describes a social class in transition. The secure and complacent leisured class lives in a world of rigid conventions in which the highest value is placed on good breeding, decorum, and conspicuous consumption. Indifferent to everything but their own elitist concerns, they were oblivious to the social changes taking place around them, such as the leveling of the classes and the mobility between them. Employing the psychological modes of William James, di Giuseppe demonstrates how being raised in such a class renders its members incapable of surviving in any other environment. At that time it was widely held that a person's character and fate are one, character, in turn, being determined by breeding and environment. The social conditioning experienced by the chief protagonist, Lily Bart, with its emphasis on witty conversation and gracious living, shapes her such that she becomes a prisoner of her class' value system. When she later becomes an impecunious orphan, her unconscious adherence to upper-crust morality does not permit her to make the moves necessary to secure her emotional and spiritual stability and her survival; instead she "accidentally on purpose" commits suicide.

Anderson and di Giuseppe show individuals as victims of social forces of a particular kind. Balance Chow's analysis of the 1988 six-part television series "He Shang" depicts an entire nation as a prisoner of its traditional value system. First, he calls attention to the overwhelming positive reaction to the negative image of China's cultural heritage. Each segment focuses on those things in China's history which have molded the modern citizen, who is characterized as backward, inflexible, and xenophobic, and by political and cultural inertia. The problems outlined, the solutions proposed, even the series itself, grew out of a movement known as the "the cultural craze" of the 1980s. Intellectuals who formed the nucleus pointed out that China's own culture has caused, and still causes, efforts at modernization to fail. To develop a modern mentality based on science and democracy, traditional values must be transformed. Not only will universal education be necessary for this, the entire country is also obligated to do some "reflective thinking" about its culture and philosophy of life. Left unchallenged, these intellectuals say, traditional forces will eventually thwart those economic and material improvements already achieved. What the series did, in effect was take the debate out of intellectual circles and go public with it, much as Martin Luther did with his *Ninety-five Theses*. The astounding success of the series alarmed the authorities, who promptly banned it. The irony of it all is that what the scriptwriters predicted would happen if the country did not reform its value system actually took place in the spring of 1989 in Tiananmen Square.

The conflict of value systems also underlines Erik Curren's essay. He argues that Ishmael Reed's representation of the black-white conflict in his *Mumbo Jumbo,* and the role he assigns to art in its resolution, defines his postmodern revolt. Reed views the racial antagonism in terms of the conflict between reasoning and feeling, spirit and flesh. In twentieth century America it manifests itself in two opposing ways of looking at the world. One is based on the dominance of reason, represented by the white establishment; it values practicality and efficiency; its repressive morality promotes according to its usefulness. The opposite system, represented by African-Americans, grows out of folk tradition and stands for the cultivation of the senses; it regards people as an end in themselves. Reed's solution for bringing the two systems into harmony is through art, which has the power to effect individual and

9

social change. In proposing art as the mediator between whites and blacks, he rejects the moderns who denied that art and society have anything in common. Reed illustrates how the process might work. He tells the story or how a plague called "Jes Grew," a metaphor for art, sweeps across the nation causing the reason-dominated white establishment to abandon hard work and efficiency in favor of singing, dancing, and cultivating the carefree life.

Some of the articles in this collection deal with the history of film and cinematic adaptations rather than with a particular event in the past. Thomas Hemmeter points out the truism that when a society writes its history some things are selected to be remembered while others are chosen to be forgotten. The same principle applies to literature and film. A case in point is the source of Alfred Hitchcock's film *Sabotage*. Up until now, virtually all critics have identified Joseph Conrad's novel *The Secret Agent* (1907) as the film's source. They have chosen to forget his 1922 play *The Secret Agent,* adapted from the novel, which might also have played a role. Hitchcock himself contributed to the confusion in that he never referred to the play, although he probably saw it—probably because it was too recent and, being a bad play, had only a short run. Hemmetter sets himself the task of refreshing our memory. By illustrating parallels between the play and the film, and by dismissing the problems of adaptation and Hitchcock's critical practice, he argues convincingly for Conrad's drama being the primary inspiration for the film. In ignoring the role of the play in the film, the critics themselves become engaged in a type of history-making or history falsification.

The practice of an author or director borrowing from the work of another is a well known if not prominent feature of literature and film Linda Anderson addresses this subject in detail, observing that the practice has become quite the fashion. It takes many forms, such as background excerpts of other works on television, pastiching of a scene, direct quotation, soundtrack sampling, or use of posters. These devices may assist the viewer in interpreting the significance of the action. In

Good Morning, Vietnam (1987) a large poster of James Dean is visible behind the rebellious hero, Adrian Cronauer, during one of his confrontations with an army officer. The poster, of course, underscores Adrian's nonconformity. Generally, borrowing serves a variety of purposes: ". . . they may help to set the tone, establish character, foreshadow upcoming actions, or serve as segues between narrative strands. . . ." More often than not this practice is purely artistic adornment, not an integral part of the narrative; such as the case with *My Stepmother is an Alien*. To teach the alien Celeste Martin how to kiss earth style, her confidant, Bag, shows kissing scenes from Casablanca, *Mr. Deeds Goes to Town*, *To Catch a Thief*, and others Celeste tries frantically to duplicate. The scenes appear to have been chosen at random, since they do not support the viewer's understanding of the action. With few exceptions, then, borrowing in cinema is done purely for the fun of it, says Anderson.

Studying cinematic adaptations of literary artifacts can serve many purposes. Patricia Santoro calls attention to how it can serve as an instructional aid. Her analysis of the screen version of Miguel Delibe's *Los santos innocentos* (1981) demonstrates the ways the verbal message is made visible. Using such technical devices as fading to white instead of black, flashbacks, surreal imagery, sound effects, and other techniques, the director succeeds in approximating and making visual the theme and message of the original text. Since the film deviates slightly from its source for the sake of a more positive tone, students can be stimulated to arrive at a clear understanding of both versions by asking why, how, and to what purpose the changes were made.

In conclusion, the editor wishes to emphasize that the arrangement of essays does not imply a statement about their quality. They are grouped according to subject. All the essays included here deal with some aspect of history whether it be tracking down the source of a film, misrepresenting the past, or dealing with the nature of storytelling itself.

NOTES

[1]Hayden White, "Historical Text as Literary Artifact," *The Writing of History*, eds. Robert H. Kamry and Henry Kozicki (Madison: University of Wisconsin Press, 1978) 46. Hereafter cited in the text as HT.

[2]Northrop Frye's categories for both genres are tragic, comic, romantic, or ironic. *Anatomy of Criticism* (New York: Atheneum, 1970) 33-34.

[3]Northrop Frye, *Fables of Identity* (New York: Harcourt, Brace, and World, 1963) 53. Hereafter cited in the text as *FI*.

[4]Claude Levi-Strauss, *The Raw and the Cooked*, trans. John and Doreen Weightman (New York: Harper and Row, 1969) 13.

[5]Levi-Strauss, *The Savage Mind*, trans. George Weidenfeld and Nicholson Ltd. (Chicago: University of Chicago Press, 1966) 261.

[6]Michel Foucault, *History of Sexuality, Volume 1: An Introduction*, trans. Robert Hurley (New York: Vintage Books, 1980) 61-62.

2. REWRITING THE RISORGIMENTO IN SICILY: VINCENZO CONSOLO'S *IL SORRISO DELL'IGNOTO MARINAIO*

T. O'Neill

VINCENZO CONSOLO'S FIRST novel, *La ferita dell'aprile*, which was first brought out by Mondadori in the "Tornasole" series (edited by the critic Niccolò Gallo and the poet Vittorio Sereni) in 1963, after a reedition by Einaude in 1977, was reprinted in late 1989 by Mondadori again. In a brief (indeed very brief) note in *Panorama* (10 December 1989), Bruno Kandler said: "Pubblicatio nel 1963, oggi è anacronistico. Ma tutto Consolo è anacronistico. Perciò va letto" (Published in 1963, today it is anachronistic. But all Consolo is anachronistic. Therefore it must be read). A short, prefatory paragraph to that anachronistic work reads as follows:

> S'intenda l'ordine l'istituto i superiori gli allievi i bastasi, di cue parla questo libro, come l'Ordine l'Istituto i Superiori gli Allievi i Bastasi. Persone, fatti, luoghi sono immaginari. Reale è il libro che dedico, con pudore, a mio padre.

(The order, the institution, the superiors, the pupils, the porters, about which this book talks, are to be understood as the Order, the Institutition, the Superiors, the Pupils, the Porters. Persons, facts, places are imaginary. What is real is the book which I dedicate, with modesty, to my father.)[1]

Repetition of the series of nouns, initially in lower case and then in upper case, is intended, surely, to stress the reality of those "Persone, fatti, luoghi" (Persons, facts, places) which in the sentence immediately following are defined as "immaginari" (imaginary). And that nexus fact-fiction (but in what relationship?) is underscored in the emphasis the author gives in the final sentence to the reality of the book. There is, in short, right from the outset in Consolo, anachronistic though he may be, an awareness that "le cose non sono come sono!" (things are not as they are).

That particular observation belongs to the Benedictine monk Giuseppe Vella, author of a forged Arab codex that demolishes baronial privilege in eighteenth-century Sicily in favor of the monarchy in Naples. Vella is co-protagonist, along with the Jacobin lawyer Francesco Paolo di Blasi, of Leonardo Sciascia's novel *Il consiglio d'Egitto*, which appeared in 1963, the same year as Consolo's first work.[2] Sciascia's novel, set in eighteenth-century Palermo and defined upon its appearance by Giancarlo Vigorelli as the "antigattopardo" (anti-leopard),[3] was intended historically to juxtapose to Don Fabrizio's vision of an unchanging Sicily (unchanging because its inhabitants, blindly thinking themselves perfect, saw no need for change),[4] a potentially revolutionary society whose revolutionary potential is neutralised on a local level by the uncovering of the plot Di Blasi is preparing, but more importantly by the forgery that Vella is elaborating, which will, more than anything, guarantee the continuance of the status quo. The Council of Egypt Vella is working on is, literally, that. It is also, as its wonderfully ambiguous title linguistically indicates, "d'Egitto" (of Egypt), but also, in popular Italian, something that is merely a figment of the imagination—a fabrication, a forgery; or, to use Sciascia's own term, an "impostura," a fraud. *Il Gattopardo* also deals at one point with an *impostura,* that of the manipulated results of the plebiscite votes at Donnafugata, but whereas in Tomasi's novel it is a minor concern for both protagonist and author (and I consciously and deliberately distinguish between them; Don Fabrizio and Giuseppe Tomasi are *not* one and the same),[5] in Sciascia's novel it is an overriding concern historically and, indeed, existentially. It is Di Blasi who, under torture, thinking of Vella, muses,

> L'abate Vella. "Ha declinato a suo modo l'impostura della vita: allegramente. . . . Non l'impostura della vita: l'impostura che è nella vita. . . . Non nella vita. . . . Ma sí, anche nella vita. . . .

> (Abbot Vella. "He spelled out the fraud of life, after his own fashion. . . . With zest. . . . Not the fraud of life, the fraud that is in life. . . . Not in life. . . . Yes, yes, in life. . . .)[6]

And it is Vella himself who while speciously, spuriously justifying his forgery to his helper, the monk Giuseppe Cammilleri, passionately dictates one of the novel's finest pages.[7]

But neither Sciascia, nor Tomasi, concerned though they may be in their own different ways with "impostura," depart essentially from traditional linear structure and chronology in their respective novels. Consolo does. It is apparent from the appendix that chronologically, although the work is essentially linear like the other two, its basic time-span, 12 September 1852–15 October 1860, is interrupted in three ways. First of all, it is interrupted by a series of general and specific references back to the Revolution of 1848 which run through the book as though to underline that *lo sbarco*, the landing of Giuseppe Garibaldi at Marsala in May 1860, and its consequences are not comprehensible without reference back to that earlier historical period. Second, it is interrupted by a number of appendices (I shall shortly return to these per se) which although concerned with the central events of the novel are in fact substantially later reconstructions of those events. Thus, for example, the *Appendice Prima* of Chapter II is in essence an extract from a lecture given in 1906 by the Sicilian historian, Francesco Guardione, on the subject matter itself of Chapter II, the uprising in Cefalú in November 1856. The chapter itself indirectly provides us, so to speak, with the "antefatto" (antecedent facts), with Interdonato's request to Mandralisca to hold a meeting in his house, a meeting obviously intended to prepare for the uprising; the appendix itself, instead, provides us with the details of the uprising and its aftermath.

Third, it is interrupted from Chapter V onwards, in spite of the specific chronological details provided by way of preface to individual chapters, by an overwhelming sense of timelessness, of time out of life, of time out of history. For example, in the opening page of Chapter V, duly dated "In Alcàra Li Fuse li 16 maggio 1860" (In Alcàra Li Fusi the 16 May 1860), the opening paragraph focuses on the day of Peppe Sirna given over to trying to extract a living from a harsh and stony land (a land which, of course, belongs to someone else, the barone Manca). Although his day is duly and regularly divided in that first paragraph with its explicit references to both "alba" (dawn) and "mezzogiorno" (midday), these clearly have no significance compared with his hope that that land may be his, "presto, domani, chi lo sa. . . ." (soon, tomorrow, who knows. . . .). It is an all-consuming idea.

> E non pensava ad altro. Ch'a questa idea antica, familiare, per cui scivolava nell'assopimento, nell'oblìo di sé nella fatica. E non sapeva piú di essere un uomo, Giusippe Sirna Papa, figlio di Giuseppe, marito a Serafina. . . . E non sapeva del luogo, dell'ora i la stagione. Solo lo stridere della zappa sulla terra e le pietre, e lui incantato, appresso, hah hah, come asino cieco dietro al cigolar di secchia della senia.

> (And he thought only of this. Only of this idea, familiar since time immemorial, by means of which he was wont to slip into drowsiness, to forget himself in his harsh labour.

And he no longer realised he was a man, Giuseppe Sirna
Papa, born in Alcàra, twenty-six years old, day-labourer,
son of Giuseppe, husband to Serafina. . . . And he knew not
the place, the hour, or the season. Only the scraping of the
hoe on the earth and the rocks, and himself mesmerized,
close by, huh huh, like a blind ass to the creaking of the
bucket).[8]

It is clear that the labourer's dream is simply that, a dream, with little or
no hope of ever being realised. This timelessness becomes absolute in
the last two chapters of the work. In Chapter VIII, "Il carcere" (The
Prison), there is no initial prefatory dating as there is in the preceding
chapters, and a solitary chronological reference in the body of the chapter is insignificant, of purely antiquarian value. Chapter IX, "Le scritte"
(The Writings), simply reproduces Mandralisca's transcriptions of the
writings on the prison walls.

The narrative text proper is interrupted, as mentioned, by a number
of appendices and it might here be useful to look at these and see what
relationship they have to the narrative proper and what light they may
throw on it. The most significant are, I believe, the two added at the end
of Chapter II. The first of these, as already mentioned, is constituted by
extracts from the historian Guardione's account of the 1856 uprising in
Cefalú; the second, instead, by extracts from Giuseppe Cesare Abba's
Noterelle d'Uno Dei Mille.[9] The juxtaposition of these two texts is
striking. The first is, as far as one can judge, a scholarly, professional
historical piece whose dominant note is its soberness; the second, not
by chance, one suspects, alternatively defined as an "intermezzo," is a
highly idealized version of Garibaldi's landing, not unlike Brancaccio
di Carpino's *Tre mesi nella Vicaria di Palermo nel 1860*, which perhaps provided Tomasi di Lampedusa with details for the figure of
Tancredi.[10] Abba and his fellow soldiers, like Tancredi, Cavriaghi, and
their fellow soldiers in *Il Gattapardo*, are for the most part well-heeled
young bourgeois or aristocrats seeking adventure. This light, frivolous
text serves by way of prologue to the violence of the facts in the chap-

ters that follow. But to return for a moment to Guardione's piece, it not only provides a contrast with Abba, it also in its unadorned sobriety contrasts with the narrative text of *Il sorriso* itself.

Consolo alone, I believe, among the moderns to have substantially appreciated and benefitted from Verga's lesson of style, has frequent recourse to "discorso libero indiretto" (free indirect speech), but the impression of impersonality, of objectivity, of the text which, to use Verga's own words, "sembrerà assersi *fatta de sé,*" (will seem *to have made itself*), is frequently negated by authorial intervention intended to point up the work's fictiveness.[11] Pages 29-30 give us a telling example. Interdonato's explanation to the two illiterate *sbirri* (constables) that the captain of the vessel "parla in metafora, la lingua della gente che vive avanti e indiretro sopra il mare, come i beduini del deserto" (speaks through metaphor, the language of people who live to and fro on the sea, like bedouins in the dessert) is followed almost immediately by the author's intervention:

> Dobbiamo ancora dire che il Bajona non sapeva leggere e che il Chinnici a decifrarlo ci metterà un anno?

> (Need we point out that Bajona did not know how to read and that Chinnici to decipher it would take a year?)

> Quindi lo riportiamo qui di sotto, avendo del lettore gran rispetto, sapendo che alle volte il temp vero e il tempo del raconto sono in disaccordo.

> (Consequently we shall report it here below, having great respect for our readers, knowing that on occasions real time and narrative time do not accord.)

The illiteracy of the constables gives a decidedly sharper focus to the literary craftsmanship of the knowing author. And that can be seen not only in the consumate poeticity of the language of the text,[12] not only in its rich "plurilinguismo" (plurilinguism), but also in its overt literary allusiveness.[13]

E mentre che il Chinnici sta leggendo con gran sforzo, noi seguiamo il nostro mercatante e il giovane garzone Palamara. . . .

(And while Chinnici is reading with great effort, let us follow our merchant and the young lad Palamara.)

That "nostro" (our). Who does not recall "il nostro Abbondio, non nobile, non ricco, coraggioso ancor meno" (our Abbondio, not noble, not rich, courageous even less) of Manzonian memory?[14] Alessandro Manzoni is literally present in the text, on page 78, with an extract in italics from towards the end of Chapter XXI of *The Betrothed,* the lines describing the peal of bells heard by the Innominato (the Unnamed) toward dawn on the day of his conversion. Why Manzoni appears directly cited in the text, I do not know. But he is not the only one. The Colonel, for example, dispatched by Garibaldi to quell the uprising in Alcàra Li Fusi, having done so departs, literally, in Dantèsque fashion: "E in cosí dire riprese il suo fatale andare" ("And with these words he continued on his fated journey"). The direct quotation, from *Inferno,* Canto V, line 22, is self-evident. And others, Latin and Italian, could be added.

Mandralisca himself in his "Memoria" to *Interdonato* (Chapter VII) questions his own ability to describe the events he has witnessed, and he does so by invoking the genuinely great writers of the past and a somewhat more mixed group of his own contemporaries.

Oh descriver potrò mai quel teatro, la spaventosa scena paratasi davanti su per le strade, i piani di quel borgo? Il genio mi ci vorria dell'Alighieri, dell'Astigian la foga, del Foscolo o del Byron la vena, dell'anglo tragediante, dell'angelo britanno il focco o la fiammante daga che scioglie d'in sul becca della penna le chine raggelate per l'orrore, o del D'Azaglio o Vittor Hugo o del Guerrazzi almen la larga prosa. . . . Di me, lassol che natura di fame, di fralezza e di baragli ha corredato, v'appagate?

(Oh shall I ever be able to describe that theatre, the dreadful scene presented o our eyes up through the streets, the levels of that hill town? The genius required of me would be that of Allighieri, of Asti's writer (Vittorio Alfieri) the passion, of Foscolo or of Byron the inspiration, of the English trage-dian, of the British angel the fire or the flaming dagger that melts on the tip of the pen the ink frozen through horror, or of D'Azeglio, of Victor Hugo or of Guerrazzi at least the wide-ranging prose. . . . With me, alas, whom nature with hunger, frailty and "baragli" [?] has endowed, would you be content?)[15]

This lack of a personally adequate language, however, has greater and more important resonance within the novel. It is hinted at in Chapter One with the names of ancient cities where Mandralisca would will-ingly have excavated had he thought he could have found there a vase, a lamp, or simply a coin: "avrebbe raspato con le mani, ginocchioni, fosse stato certo di trovare un vaso, una lucerna o solo una moneta" (he would have scratched around with his hands, down on his knees, had he been certain of finding a vase, a lamp or only a coin) (*SI* 4). But, the text continues: "Ma quelle, in vero, non sono ormai che nomi, somma-mente vaghi, suoni, sogni." (But those, in truth, are now but names, supremely beautiful, sounds, dreams) (*SI* 4). And to understand the full significance of this we must turn, after the tragic events of Alcàra Li Fusi, to Chapter VI, the letter of Mandralisca to Interdonato, where, talking of the most sacred and elementary rights of man, "la terra e il pane, la salute e l'amore, la pace la goija e l'istruzione" (land and bread, health and love, peace joy and education) (*SI* 98) he asks why the have-nots should understand these words as he and his do: "perchè devono intender quelle parole a modo nostro?" (why should they under-stand these words as we do?) (*SI* 98). To which he at once replies,

Ah, tempo verrà in cui da soli conquisteranno que' valori,
ed essi li chiameranno con parole nuove, vere per loro, e

giocoforza anche per noi, vere perchè i nomi saranno intier-
amente riempiti dalle cose.

(Ah, the time will come when by themselves they will acquire these values, and they will talk of them with new
words, true for them, and perforce also for us, true because
the names will be entirely filled out with the things.) (*SI* 98)

The starting point here, if I am not mistaken, is Luigi Pirandello's
essay on Verga, but we need not have recourse to such illustrious
names, for Consolo's own text, it is reasonable to assert, is concerned
specifically with a world expressing itself through language.[16] Two
incidents, or, more precisely, one incident and two commentaries in the
text are illuminating. The incident is the encounter in Chapter IV
between Mandralisca and the young prisoner chained up in the
courtyard of the Granza Maniforti castle at Sant'Agata di Militello. To
the questions put to him by Mandralisca in his language, his privileged
Italian, the prisoner replies in his own, the language of San Fratello.
Maniforti's servant illuminates this in the first instance when, in
response to Mandralisca's question as to where the prisoner comes
from, he says, "Ah. Sanfratellano Dio ne scansi! Gente selvaggia,
diversa, curiosa. E parlano 'na lingua stramba, forestiera." (Ah. From
San Fratello, God protect us! Wild people, different, curious. And they
speak a strange, foreign tongue) (*SI* 81).

Consolo provides ("privileges" might perhaps be a more accurate
term) his reader with an Italian translation in footnotes. These footnotes
are almost the only ones in the text. As for the Spanish of Goya, the
Latin version of Exodus, the transliterated but not translated Greek of
Stephen of Byzantium, the reader must make his or her own arrangement, but he or she will have not difficulty in doing so for Consolo's
text. Although these tongues are, in Dantesque fashion, "diverse"
(diverse), they are nevertheless civilized; they are not, to remain with
Alighieri Dante (*Inferno,* III. 25), "orribili favelle" (horrible languages)
beyond the pale of human, that is to say civil, social comprehension like

the tongue spoken by the prisoner and his like, "na lingua stranba, forestiera" (a strange, foreign tongue).

In immediate and sharp juxtaposition to these remarks of the servant, there follows in the next paragraph (pages 81-82 of the Einaudi text) Mandralisca's own, more learned and philologically more accurate thoughts on this tongue of one of the villages of the Val Dèmone; but here too the rhetorical question that parenthetically closes the paragraph, in contrast to the Greek of its first part, seems to suggest that if the village has had a history, it has been a history of regress, a downward spiral reflected in the shift away from the island's original language, the language of Plato, of Aristotle to his "lingua stramba, forestiera" spoken by a people who are "selvaggia, diversa, curiosa" (wild, different, curious).

But if Mandralisca is, in the words of *Interdonato*, "un uomo che ha le capacità di mente e di cuore per poter capire" (a man who has the ability of mind and heart to be able to understand) (*SI* 98), it will require the experience of the aftermath of Alcàra Li Fusi to provoke him into action, but, prior to this, he will meditate. In Chapter VI, arguably the most important for an understanding of the work, Consolo/Mandralisca, like Sciascia/Vella in *Il Consiglio* (that same page 59 cited in Note 7), concludes that the pen is mightier than the sword, but, in a Catch-22 situation, the pen, the language that liberates, may continue to repress, continue to enslave. Mandralisca's letter may very well be intended, as he says, "quale mezzo conoscitivo indipendente, obiettivo e franco" (as an independent, objective, and frank means towards knowledge) (*SI* 96), but surely we must, regardless of his honourable and honest intentions, treat with caution his claim to independence and objectivity (that same independence and objectivity we must assume present also in the paper of the professional historian Guardione) if, at the end of the very same paragraph in which he lays claims to these, in answer to his own rhetorical question, "E cos'è stata la storia sin qui. . . ? ("And what has History been up until now. . . ?), he replies: "Una scrittura continua di privilegiati" ("A continuous writing by privileged people").

Mandralisca himself is only too well aware of the impossibility of his task:

> Sarà possibile questo scarto di voce e di persona? No, no! Che per quanto l'intenzione e il cuore sian disposti, troppi vizi ci nutriamo dentro, storture, magagne, per nascita, cultura e per il censo. Ed è impostura mai sempre la scrittura di noi cosiddetti illuminati. . . ."

> (Will it be possible to eliminate this disparity between voice and person? No, no! for no matter how well-intentioned the heart be, too many vices do we nourish within ourselves, mistaken ideas, flaws of birth, culture, socio-economic standing.) (*SI* 97)

Or yet again more clearly, at the beginning Chapter VII.

> La contraddizione infine nel ritrovarmi a dire, com'io dissi, dell'impossibilità di scrivere se non si vuol tradire, creare l'impostura, e la necessità insieme e l'impellenza a farlo.

> (The contradiction in the last analysis of finding myself in the situation of having to talk, as I said, about the impossibility of writing if one does not wish to betray, to create fraud, and at the same time the necessity and the compulsion to do it.) (*SI* 103)

The language of San Fratello is not, Mandralisca realizes, "na lingua stramba, forestiera" (a strange, foreign tongue), as Maniforti's servant in his ignorance believed it to be; but, instead, a "lingua bellissima, romanza o mediolantina, rimasta intatta per un millennio sano" (most beautiful tongue, romance or medieval Latin, remained intact for a full thousand years) (*SI* 97). More striking than the superlative "bellissima," intended, no doubt, to contrast with the strangeness and foreignness of the uneducated definition of the servant, are the other two adjectives: that thousand year period defined as "sano" (literally "healthy") and the language throughout that period which has remained "intatto"—intact because, clearly, untouched by history. But, we might legitimately ask ourselves, what sort of health is it which allows for no growth, no development, no progress?

In his *Epoche della lingua italiana,* Ugo Foscolo constantly compared Italian to Greek—Greek, his mother tongue, being for him, axiomatically, the most beautiful of tongues—Greek first, Italian, so to speak, a close second.[17] A like linguistic rationale underpins Consolo's text, but he through the intermediary of Mandralisca extends that mark of nobility to the language of San Fratello: "lingua bellissima." And yet, not only is *Il sorriso* not written in that tongue, but even of the twelve "scritte" (writings) that go to make up Chapter IX, only the final one is given to us in it. The proclamation of the pro-dictator Mordini, "Italiani della Sicilia!" (Italians of Sicily), twice repeated in the novel's very last page, brings home to us that Garibaldi's victory is also a linguistic victory that necessarily entails the destruction of other languages, of other cultures, all of which threatened in their own ways to undermine the unity in the process of being achieved. Consolo, an exquisitely Sicilian writer, can give us at most that single page in San Fratellano, but it is lost amid the baroque richness of the Italian in which he writes. The success that he enjoys as a writer in Italian only serves tragically to heighten his failure and our failure to write the real history of the Risorgimento in Sicily in its own language.[18]

APPENDIX

I.   Il sorriso dell'ignoto marinaio

12 settembre 1852.

Festa del Santissimo nome di Maria (N.B. This date appears not in the original Einaudi edition, but in the Mondadori test of 1987, p.3).

LA SERA DEL 27 OTTOBRE 1852 (p.11)

APPENDICE PRIMA

Lettera di Enrico Pirajna barone di Mandralisca al baron Andrea Bivona de servire da prefazione al "Cataologo dei molluschi terre—stri e fluviatili delle Madonie e luoghi adiacenti"— Palermo—Dalla stamperia Dretea—via dell'Albergaria num. 240- 1840(p.22).

APPENDICE SECONDA

Nota-di-talune specie di molluschi terrestri e fluviatili di Sicilia— Di Enrico Pirajno—barone di Mandralisca—Palermo—Estratto dal Giornale setterario—num. 230—1842 (p 25).

IL L'albero delle quattro arance

Lipari li 8 Novembre 1856 (p. 32)

-No, no . . . Sapete bene che mi riferisco al quarantotto . . . . (p. 34) [1848].

APPENDICE PRIMA

Francesco Guardione: "Il moto politico di Cefalú nel 1856" (Lettura tenuta il di 25 novembre 1906 in Cefalú nella chiesa della Mercede, ove sorge il monumento a Salvatore Spinuzza). Cefalú nella chiesa della Merceda, ove sorge il monumento a Salvatore Spinuzza). Cefalú—Tipografia Sav. Gussio- 1907 (p. 47).

III. Morti sacrata

In Alcàra Li Fusi sopra i Nèbrodi li 13 di maggio 1860 (p. 59)

"Brigante [Garibaldi]. Nemico di Dio e di Sua Maestà il re Dio-guardi. Sbarca in Sicilia e avviene un quarantotto . . . ." (p. 64) [1848].

IV. Val Dèmone

In Sant'Agata di Militello li 15 maggio 1860. (p. 69)

Vi conosciamo! Deste ricetto nella casa vostra nel novembre dell'anno scorso ch'è trascorso a pericolosi gaglioffi e orditori di sommossee e rivolte contro la Sacra Maestà e l'Ordine Sovrano. Nel '48 foste deputato conquel Ruggiero Settimo che si nasconde a Malta, presidente d'un regno di burletta, e mai ritrattaste la fede vostra nel sovvertimento. Mandralisca, questi son solo i capi principali—(p 77).

V. Il Vespero

In Alcàra Li Fusi li 16 maggio 1860 (p 85)

VI. Letera di Enrico Pirajno all'avvocato Giovanni Interdonato come preambolo a la memoria sui fatti d'Alcàra Li Fusi

Cefalú li 9 ottobre 1860. (p. 95)

"Vogliate riandare con la memoria a una serata di novembre del 1856. . . ." (p 95);

"sappiate che si tratta degli atroci fatti succedutisi in Alcàra Li Fusi sopra i Nèbrodi, in Val Dèmone, il di 17 maggio e seguenti or ora scorsi, e di cui lo scrivente si è trovato a esser, ahil, in parte spettatore per fortuito caso o per destino (pp. 95-6).

VII. Memoria

Cefalú li 15 ottobre 1860 (p. 103)

"Il sedici di maggio recavami in Alcàra, ospite del barone Crescenzio Manca, per quell'idea strologa, dannata, della ricerca e catalogazione di lumache, e il diciasette dunque, l'"Ascensione, successe in quella piazza il quarantotto. . . ." (p. 104) [1848].

"Ventiquattro di giugno, San Giovanni, le cinque ore dopo mezzogiorno" (p. 105).

"Ventiquattro di giugno, San Giovanni, era per gli Alcaresi la festa del Mozzone, e festeggiare soleano nei quartieri quelle piccole brocche e i germogli, con canti e danze, fino a notte alta. Si scioglievano allora le inimecizie, s'intrecciavano gli amori, i comparaggi (p. 108).

VIII. Il carcere

"Appellasi, Sant'Agata, di Militello, poichè fino al recente 1857 non ebbe autonomia di comune, ma dipendeva in tutto da quell'altro" (p. 115).

IX Le scritte

APPENDICE PRIMA

Una deliberazione celebre almeno come paradosso ovvero L'assassinio in trionfo

Palermo—Stamperia Carini all'insegna di Guttemberg—Entrata del Teatro Nazionale a S. Ferdinando—Unico piano a destra—[December] 1860 (p. 134).

APPENDICE SECONDA

NOTES

[1]Vincenzo Consolo, *La Ferita dell'Aprile* (Milan: Einaudi, 1977) 2, translation mine.

[2]Leonardo Sciascia, *Il Consiglio d'Egitto,* (Milan: Einaudi, 1963) 12. *The Council of Egypt,*trans. Adrienne Foulke (Manchester and New York: Carcanet Press Limited, 1988) 5. On this particular text, see Jo Ann Cannon, *Postmodern Italian Fiction: The Crisis of Reason in*

Calvino, Eco, Sciascia, Malerba (Fairleigh Dickinson University Press, 1989) esp. 40–59.

[3]The review was published in *Tempo* (23 February 1963).

[4]See Giuseppe Tomasi di Lampedusa, *Il Gattopardo* (Milan: Giangiacomo Feltrinelli editore, 1959) 216–17: "Uno di loro, poi, mi chiese che cosa veramenta venissero a fare qui in Sicilia quei volontari italiani. *They are coming to teach us good manners,* risposi. *"But they wont succeed, because we are gods."* Vengono per insegnarci le buone creanze ma non lo potranno fare, perché noi siamo déi. Credo che non comprendessero, ma risero e se ne andarono. Cosí rispondo anche a lei, caro Chevalley: i Siciliani non vorranno mai migliorare per la semplice ragione che credono di essere perfett . . ."" (""Then one of them asked me what those Italian volunteers were really coming to do in Sicily. *They are coming to teach us good manners!'* I replied in English. *'But they won't succeed, because we are gods.'* I don't think they understood, but they laughed and went off. That is my answer to you too, my dear Chevalley; the Sicilians never want to improve for the simple reason that they think themselves perfect . . .'") in Giuseppe Tomasi di Lampedusa, *The Leopard with a Memory and Two Stories,* *t*rans. Archibald Colquhoun (London: Collins Harvill, 1986) 146–47.

[5]See my "Tomasi di Lampedusa e Bassani: Affinità Elettive," in *Filologia Italiana,* Anno XIV, n. 15 (Ankara 1987): 163-81.

[6]*Il Consiglia d'Egitto, cit.,* 159.*The Council of Egypt, cit.,* 184.

[7]See in *Il Consiglio,* cit., 59: "Tutta un'impostura. La storia non esiste. Forse che esistono le generazioni di foglie che sono andate via da quell'albero, un autunno appresso all'altro? Esiste l'albero, esistono le sue foglie nuove: poi anche queste foglie se ne andranno; e a un certo punto se ne andrià anche l'albero: in fumo, in cenera. La storia delle foglie, la storia dell'albero. Fesserie! Se ogni foglia scrivesse la sua storia, se quest'albero scrivesse la sua, allora diremmo: eh si, la storia. . . . Vostro nonno ha scritto la sua storia? E vostro patre? E il mio? E i nostri avoli e trisavoli? . . . Sono discesi a marcire nella terra né piú e némeno che come foglie, senza lasciare storia. . . . C'è ancora l'al-

bero, si, ci siamo noi come foglie nuove . . . E ce ne andremo anche
noi. . . . L'albero che resterà, se resterà può anch'essere segato ramo a
ramo: i re, i viceré, i papi, i capitani; i grandi, insomma . . . Facciamone
un po' di fuoco, un op' di fumo: ad illudere i popoli, le nazioni, l'uman-
ità vivente. . . . La storia! E mio padre? E vostro padre? E il gorgoglio
delle loro viscere vuote? E la voce della loro fame? Credete che si sen-
tirà, nella storia? Che ci sarà uno storico che avrà orecchio talmente
fino da sentirlo?" (and in *The Council of Egypt, cit.*, 64-65: "'It's all
fraud. History does anot exist. Perhaps you think the generations of
leaves that have dropped from that tree autumn after autumn still exist?
The tree exists; its new leaves exist; but these leaves will also fall; in
time, the tree itself will disappear—in smoke, in ashes. A history of
those leaves? A history of that tree? Nonsense! If every leaf were to
write its history, if the tree were to write its history, then we would say,
'Ah yes, this is history. . . .' Your grandfather, did he write his history?
Or your father? Or mine? Or our great-grandfathers or our great-great-
grandfathers? They went down into the earth to rot, no more and no
less, like the leaves, and they left no history of themselves. . . . The tree
is still there, yes, and we are its new leaves. And we will fall, too. . . .
The tree that will remain, if it does remain, can also be sawed down,
limb by limb: kings, viceroys, popes, generals, the great ones, that
is. . . . What we are making, you and I, is a little fire, a little smoke with
those limbs, in order to beguile people, whole nations—every living
human being. . . . History! What about my father? What about your father? And the rumbling of their empty bellies, the voice of their
hunger? Do you believe this will be heard in history? That there will be
a historian with an ear keen enough to hear?'")

[8]Vincenzo Consolo, *Il sorriso dell'ignoto marinaio* (Turin:
Eianu—di, 1976) 85, translation mine. I have been unable to ascertain
the meaning of the term "sènia."

[9]First published by Zanichelli in Bologna in 1880. In 1910, fifty
years after Garibaldi's landing, Abba promised the king a second version after a return visit to Sicily by him.

[10]A translation of the Italian text by John Parris was brought out by The Folio Society in London in 1968 under the title *The Flight for Freedom: Palermo, 1960.* See page 17 of the introduction for the suggestion linking it to *Il Gattopardo.* Corroboration of this given by Gioacchino Lanza Tomasi, the author's adopted son, in his Preface to Giuseppe Tomasi di Lampedusa, *Il Gattopardo. Edizione conforme al manoscritto del 1957* (Milan: Feltrinelli, 1969) XVIII-XIX, where he also recognizes that he himself in part served as model for the figure of Tancredi.

[11]The oft-quoted phrase is to be found in the letter to Salvatore Farina which prefaced the short story "L'amante di Gramigna" ("Gramigna's lover") in the collection entitled *Vita dei campi.* The translation quoted is D. H. Lawrence's.

[12]"Sul pavimento a ciottoli impetrato ricoverti da scivoloso musco e da lichene, tra le pareti e la volta del cunicolo levigate a malta, jisso, a tratti come spalmate di madreperla pesta, pasta di vetro, vernice d'India o lacca, lustre come porcellana della Cina, porpora in sulle labbra, sfumante in dentro verso il rosa e il latte, a tratti gonfie e scalcinate per penetrazione d'acqua, che dalla volta gocciola a cannolicchi càlcichi, deturpate da muffe brune e verdi, fiori di salnitro e capelvenere a cascate dalle crepe: luogo di delizie *origine,* rifugio di frescura pel principe e la corte lungo i tre giorni infacati di scirocco, come le cascatelle della Zisa, i laghi e i ruscelli a Maredolce . . ." (118-19). I cite the passage untranslated since my primary intention here is simply to indicate the high frequency of alliteration as one of the more self-evident aspects of the text's poeticity.

[13]In addition to the intrinsically baroque and regional Italian of the text, we should also consider its various quotations in Latin, Greek, and Spanish, not to mention the dialect of the Val Dèmone.

[14]Alessandro Manzoni, *I promessi sposi* (Milan: Feltrinelli, 1965) 21, translation mine.

[15]*Il sorriso dell'ignoto marinaio, cit.,* 105, translation mine. I have been unable, here too, to ascertain the meaning of "baragli."

[16]See his "Discorso alla Reale Accademia d'Italia" of 3 December 1931 in Luigi Pirandello, *Saggi, poesie, scritte varie* (Milan: Mondadori, 1977) 391, where he makes a distinction between a "stile di cose" and a "stile di parole."

[17]See my "Foscolo's *Epoche;* The Greek Connection," in T. O'Neill, *The Shared Horizon* (Dublin: Irish Academic Press, 1990) 105-21.

[18]See Geoffrey Hull, "Idealist Nationalism and Linguistic Dogma in Italy," *The Shared Horizon,* 149-83.

3. FROM PRINTED PAGE TO SCREEN: "THE VOYAGE OF CHARLES DARWIN"

Julie S. Gibert

HISTORIANS DECRY THE DECLINE of historical interest in contemporary American society. They bemoan the fact that students in many (though mercifully not in all) cases study history not because it is interesting but because it is required. The problem of student apathy seems to reflect a general trend—journalists habitually ignoring the historical background of modern issues, and legislators pursuing their programs with little reference to past experience.

These plaints about the decline of history can be easily countered. A glance at the television listings reveals that history can be marketed even in today's presentist society. Whether in the guise of romance (as in *Gone with the Wind* and its host of imitators) or in the form of documentaries such as "Eyes on the Prize" and "Vietnam: a Television History," images of the past attract viewers.

In this paper, through an analysis of one television drama—the seven-part series "The Voyage of Charles Darwin"—I examine the relationship between history on video and more traditional written and classroom history.[1] My comparison of the Time-Life series with both primary and secondary written accounts of Darwin's career suggests that the question of accuracy in "video history" is not, as viewers and critics often suppose, simply a question of proper chronology or of the inclusion of relevant historical characters and incidents. It is also a question of the interpretation and portrayal of much broader contexts and themes.

"The Voyage of Charles Darwin" does not pretend, of course, to relate the history of Victorian England or even to offer a thorough discussion of the role of scientific investigation in Victorian England. In evaluating it one must remember that it is, quite simply, a filmed biography of Charles Darwin. Or perhaps we should call it a filmed *autobiography*, since the series is unified and in some sections extensively narrated by extracts from Darwin's own published Autobiography.[2]

Nevertheless, if only because of the necessity to place Darwin in a visually convincing setting, to select interesting scenes to carry his story forward, and to surround him with supporting characters, the teleplay must, whether intentionally or inadvertently, present an interpretation of Darwin's place in that society.

Viewed in its entirety, "The Voyage of Charles Darwin" presents its central character as the lone representative of science in a hostile or at best indifferent world. This depiction differs sharply from that offered by standard written works, notably Michael Ruse's *The Darwinian Revolution* and Gertrude Himmelfarb's *Darwin and the Darwinian Revolution*.[3] Ruse's and Himmelfarb's books, both likely choices as texts in courses on Victorian history or on the history of science, depict Darwin as a member of the active scientific fraternity of a rapidly modernizing state.

The television series' interpretation appears clearly in its treatment of Darwin's background, early life, and education. The series repeatedly portrays Darwin as a dilettante, a clumsy hobbyist who, until undertaking his voyage on the *Beagle,* has no intention of or potential for becoming the most prominent naturalist of his day.

This impression arises first through the choice of evidence from Darwin's autobiography. Through a series of voiceovers taken from Darwin's own published recollections the viewer hears, early in the first episode and repeatedly throughout the series, that Darwin "was considered by all my masters and by my father as a very ordinary boy, rather below the common standard in intellect." Also in the first episode, which concentrates on Darwin's educational experiences, the viewer learns—again from Darwin himself—that "during the three years which I spent at Cambridge my time was wasted."

Inevitably, of course, in the transformation from print to the screen, from the lengthy *Autobiography* to a seven-hour TV miniseries, some things must be left out. It is revealing to see just what aspects of Darwin's educational history were omitted from the teleplay. Significantly, the script does not include Darwin's statement that "the passion for collecting which leads a man to be a systematic naturalist . . . was very strong in me," or any reference to the chemical studies and experiments that Darwin and his brother carried on in their youth (*AC* 6, 11).

The impression of Darwin as a lazy student who gained little benefit from his formal education is reinforced by the portrayal of his tenure at Edinburgh University, where he undertook medical training in 1825, presented as a fiasco. The teleplay gives the impression that Darwin left medical school after his first sight of blood in the operating room. In the series' only Edinburgh scene, we see Darwin seated in the gallery of an old-fashioned operating theatre. A surgeon, clad in a bloody apron, is about to amputate his unanesthetized patient's leg. At the surgeon's first cut, Darwin claps his hand to his mouth and runs out of the room and down a narrow stone staircase into the street. In the next scene, Darwin is home in Shrewsbury, discussing alternative career choices with his exasperated father. Neither action nor narration reveals that Darwin actually spent two years attending medical, botanical, and geological lectures in Edinburgh, or that he participated in several prominent scientific societies there (*AC* 10-15).

The viewer is thus encouraged to believe that until Darwin set out on the HMS *Beagle* was entirely untrained in scientific lore and method. The only hints of Darwin's eventual career are occasional references to his habit of observing animals and collecting beetles—avocations dismissed by Darwin's father as useless and self-indulgent, and which his Cambridge friends regarded as nothing more than amusing eccentricities that occasionally interfere with the real student business of drinking and gambling.

As we've seen, even a brief comparison of the teleplay with Darwin's *Autobiography* suggests that viewers aren't getting the whole story. A more specific comparison with Michael Ruse's summary of Darwin's scientific career reinforces that impression. Ruse concedes that Darwin's academic career ". . . was not distinguished," and that "the obvious conclusion . . . is that with this kind of background Darwin would be little more than a dilettante" (*DR* 32). He disputes this interpretation, however, saying "there are good reasons to believe that Darwin became as professional as any scientist at that time" (*DR* 32). In supporting his interpretation Ruse relies upon evidence absent from the television account. He speaks, for example, of Darwin's early chemical experiments and of the influence of Darwin's scientist grandfather, Erasmus Darwin, whose *Zoonomia* Darwin undoubtedly read during his adolescence.[4] Ruse, like other writers on Darwin, concentrates also on the fact that in Edinburgh and Cambridge Darwin became friendly with several of the most eminent scientists of the early nineteenth century (*DR* 32-34, 161).

In depicting Darwin's university career, the series seems almost deliberately to minimize the importance of Darwin's university contacts. We've already seen what happened to his Edinburgh sojourn. The portrayal of his Cambridge years seems more thorough, occupying a good chunk of one episode. The episode focuses on Darwin's friendship with the naturalist John Henslow, a man who most authors agree had great influence on Darwin's career. The way the television series treats Henslow doesn't introduce the idea of Darwin's membership in a community; rather, it reinforces the viewer's initial impression of Darwin as a dilettante.

The series remains true to historical accounts by setting the first meeting of Darwin and Henslow at one of Henslow's public lectures at the botanical gardens. The direction of the scene, however, influences the viewer's reaction to Henslow. First, Darwin seems to have merely dropped in at the lecture with his cousin—the episode is apparently a Sunday afternoon outing with no academic purpose whatsoever. The church-social atmosphere is enhanced by the characters' frequent references to Henslow being a clergyman, and not a professional scientist. The series ignores the fact that Henslow was Professor of Botany at Cambridge, and that his lectures were a semi-official part of the Cambridge curriculum (*DR* 23). We know from official records that Darwin didn't just drop in on Henslow's lecture—he attended the lectures regularly, and what's more, he paid to attend, as did many undergraduates and members of the Cambridge scientific community (*DR* 33). Furthermore, most of the extras in the scene—presumably members of Henslow's usual audience—are demurely chattering Victorian ladies, complete with bonnets and reticules. Darwin's is the only academic gown to be seen.

A voiceover tells the viewer that Darwin soon became known as "the man who walks with Henslow," a remark that effectively conveys the idea that Henslow was a well-known figure around Cambridge, but that tells the viewer little about the nature of his reputation or position in the city. From the manner in which his lecture is presented and from the nature of his remarks to Darwin later in the episode, a viewer might easily be led to believe that Henslow was a prominent local clergyman with a well-known and rather eccentric taste for bug-collecting. Nothing in the television portrayal prepares the viewer for the sudden information that this mild-mannered man has strong enough influence to get young Darwin the post of ship's naturalist on the HMS *Beagle*.

Other accounts tell us that Henslow was far from being an accidental intruder and influence upon young Darwin's aspirations and interests. On the contrary, he was a leader in the busy scientific circle centered in Cambridge. His weekly lectures were an important part of the scientific life of the university city, a serious academic event often attended by prominent academics and scientists such as Adam Sedgwick, Professor of Geology and a major student of fossils, and William Whewell, Professor of Mineralogy and an important writer on scientific method (*DR* 23). Clearly, Darwin's growing reputation as "the man who walks with Henslow" marked his membership in recognized and eminent scientific circles (*DD* 43).

The television series' treatment of Henslow as a kindly dilettante is a vivid example of the treatment of the scientific community in general in "The Voyage of Charles Darwin." Just as Henslow's membership in the academic scientific group is not clearly established, the very existence of such a community is left untouched. The great scientists of the early and mid-nineteenth century are only rarely mentioned in the series, and when they do appear their contributions to science are never clearly explained. This tendency appears clearly in the series' introduction of Charles Lyell's classic and influential *Principles of Geology*.[5] Although most accounts state simply that Darwin took the book on his voyage—probably at the urging of Henslow (*DD* 96)—in the series Darwin receives Lyell's first volume as a *bon voyage* gift from the eminently conservative and traditional Captain Fitzroy. Fitzroy casually offers it to Darwin, remarking that it has just come out. Darwin replies that he has heard of the *Principles,* but has not yet read it. Nothing in their conversation tells the viewer that Lyell's work took a strikingly original approach to the study of the earth's history, or that it was destined to have a profound influence on Darwin's own theories (*DD* 82-106, *DR* 40-56). At no point in the series is the book mentioned again, and the viewer might easily be led to believe that Lyell's *Principles* was merely the most recent textbook on geology. Even in the last episode of the series, when Lyell himself appears as an important but somewhat reluctant supporter of the theory of natural selection, the viewer is told nothing about Lyell's own struggles with the "mystery of mysteries" (*DR* 75-93).

The manner of Lyell's appearance further reinforces the viewer's impression of him as a conventional figure. He appears for the first time in a book-lined Cambridge study, pouring sherry from a crystal decanter and warning Darwin that it would be heretical to suggest any change in the earth's species. The setting is accurate in that it is a faithful portrayal of a nineteenth-century gentleman's study, but to twentieth-century viewers, accustomed to thinking of science as an activity which takes place in sterile laboratories, the scene visually reinforces the idea that Lyell and his colleagues are obscure and rather quaint dilettantes.

Ruse, Himmelfarb, and other writers argue that Darwinism was the product of many minds—including Darwin, Whewell, Lyell, and many others. The television treatment, by contrast, seems to express a belief that Charles Darwin, assisted only by eccentric amateurs and dry conventional textbooks, magically arrived at the theory of natural selection. Other scientists, like Lyell, appear only in episode seven, after Darwin's ideas have fully evolved. They appear, therefore, as followers of Darwin rather than the mentors they actually were.

I have noted, up to now, mainly the absence of certain facts and ideas from the series. What about the more positive aspect—what *is* there? The idea that Darwin grew up and arrived at his earthshaking theory without the assistance of a scientific circle or of any previous research or theory is conveyed not only by the absence of any discussion of the scientific community in the series, but also by the frequent repetition of Darwin's own statement that "the voyage of the *Beagle* has been by far the most important event in my life, and has determined my whole career" (*AC* 28). This phrase from the *Autobiography* is repeated at least once per episode—a repetition that echoes the basic emphasis of the series. Of seven episodes, only one is devoted to events that occurred after Darwin's return from South America.

This emphasis on the *Beagle* voyage betrays one of the teleplay's most basic assumptions, the idea that Darwin's ideas arose purely from his own experiences, particularly in the Galapagos Islands, and not from any experiences during his years in England or from any interaction with other scientists. The series is not concerned, for example, with the development of Darwin's basic idea of natural selection after his return to England or with the subtle alterations wrought by his voracious reading and by frequent contact with other biologists, botanists, and geologists. To return to the subject of omissions for the moment, it is interesting to note that not once in the series is Darwin pictured reading a book or attending a scientific meeting.

The series' frequent quotation of Darwin's statement about the *Beagle* voyage is not at all inaccurate. Darwin does, in his *Autobiography*, speak of the trip as the pivotal event in his career. But the series does not discuss the role of that round-the-world voyage as thoroughly as does the *Autobiography* or as do writers like Ruse and Himmelfarb. These written sources spell out carefully the many diverse interests and experiences that eventually led to Darwin's insight—for example, his early scientific reading and training, his early geological field work in Wales, and his vast reading after the end of the voyage. By choosing to devote time and attention to such details, Ruse presents Darwin's ideas as a complex patchwork of theories built up gradually over the course of a lifetime. By omitting Darwin's other experiences or undercutting their significance while constantly stressing the importance of the *Beagle* trip, the television scriptwriter presents the theory of natural selection as the result of a lone man's accidental inspiration.

The series builds a vivid picture of Darwin's relationship to the society in which he lived and worked. Darwin, the scientist, is throughout the series presented as a loner, a rebel who until the publication of *The Origin of the Species* was unsupported and unaided by fellow scientists in his search for the secrets of life and speciation.[6] As we have seen, this picture tends to ignore the existence of the scientific community and to contradict Ruse's argument that Darwin was from his early years a member of the scientific establishment of his day. It also gives a very definite picture of Victorian English society and culture—a picture that once again contradicts Ruse's account and indeed contradicts most modern scholarship on Victorian England. Throughout the series Darwin, having already been established in the viewer's mind as a maverick and a misfit, is placed in direct and heroic opposition to the rigidly conservative and straightlaced Victorian mind. The conflict between Darwin and his society appears clearly in the series' account of the *Beagle* voyage. Several incidents during the voyage set Darwin up as the voice of modernism and scientific realism in contradiction to the traditional "Victorian" ethical and religious creed.

This tendency to isolate Charles Darwin appears vividly in the teleplay's recounting of his first encounter with slavery in the Caribbean. Young Charles, faced with the spectacle of a planter who orders his slaves around as though they were beasts of burden, and who callously separates mothers from children during a visit to the slave market, voices his horror at the idea that one man should own another or that cruel treatment should be justified solely on the basis of race. Significantly, he is alone in his opposition to slavery. At the planter's home he is surrounded by slaveowners who are convinced of the righteousness of their way of life. Back on the *Beagle,* he gets little sympathy from his shipmates, and in fact stumbles into a serious argument with Captain Fitzroy over the issue of slavery. It is not surprising that some people should disapprove of Darwin's views, but given that the United Kingdom abolished the slave trade in 1807 and the institution of slavery in 1833, it is likely that Darwin would have encountered some sympathy from other young officers or perhaps from the evangelical missionary who was his shipmate on the Beagle. Some historians, including Gertrude Himmelfarb, argue that Fitzroy's anger was directed at Darwin's lack of respect for authority, not at his opposition to slavery (*DD* 62). In a complete historical account, Darwin's views on slavery would appear as part of a well-established reforming tradition. In the series, the slavery incident serves only to set Darwin apart from his compatriots and contemporaries. The viewer, who has already been led to see Darwin as a bungling dilettante, is now encouraged to regard him as a radical iconoclast.

This early argument between Fitzroy and Darwin is merely one expression of a theme of conflict that runs throughout the series. From the beginning of the first episode, it is clear that Fitzroy will be the second most important character in the drama of Charles Darwin, and that his views and activities will be important points of focus. The construction of the first episode makes this relationship clear. Although almost all of the action of the episode takes place before the meeting of Darwin and Fitzroy, and indeed before Darwin even hears about the *Beagle*, scenes depicting Fitzroy's experiences alternate with those portraying Darwin's preparation for the trip. This structure, implying that Darwin and Fitzroy are somehow parallel characters, establishes an important pattern; Fitzroy, in television terms, is the costar of the series. We learn, one way and another, almost as much about Fitzroy as we do about Darwin. To give an example, in the sixth episode we see Darwin, recently returned from his five-year mission, proposing to his cousin Sophia Wedgwood. In the next scene we see, not Darwin's wedding, but a conversation between Fitzroy and a former shipmate. In that scene Fitzroy is being congratulated on his recent marriage. The attention given to Fitzroy in the first episode and then again in the final segment when the directors devote several minutes to a Parlimentary quarrel which, although important to the story of Fitzroy, is utterly irrelevant to the story of Darwin, keeps Fitzroy's character in the viewer's mind and focuses the viewer's attention on his attitudes and utterances.

From his first appearance on the *Beagle* and through his suicide in the last episode Fitzroy is characterized as an archetypal Victorian. He supports white supremacy in his acceptance of slavery and in his eagerness to adopt and "civilize" three young Tierra del Fuegans. He treasures the hierarchical organization of society and the power of the landed classes in English political life. He is morally upright to the point of priggishness. Most of all, he is fervently and rigidly devoted to the literal interpretation of the Bible and opposed to any scientific theory or speculation which threatens that view. Fitzroy's frequent contradictions of and rebukes to Darwin serve to remind the viewer again and again that Darwin will one day challenge the foundations of Fitzroy's beliefs and shake his stable and confident society to its roots. When Fitzroy slits his throat, apparently as an expression of pain and remorse over Darwin's blasphemies, it is difficult for the viewer not to perceive the incident as a symbol of the death of the old, pre-evolutionary, non-scientific world in the face of Darwin's dazzling discoveries. One of Darwin's friends even refers to Fitzroy as a dinosaur.

The television portrayal of Darwin's unstable friendship is accurate; contemporary accounts, including Darwin's journals and autobiography, indicate that Fitzroy was rigidly conservative and often harshly judgmental. He and Darwin did differ politically—Darwin's family was staunchly Whig, and Fitzroy's extremely Tory, so Tory as to be opposed to the 1832 reform bill. Fitzroy and Darwin had public and apparently quite vicious arguments (*DD* 60-63). Most writers, though, including Darwin himself, treat Fitzroy as a fairly minor character in Darwin's life. The television writers' decision to emphasize his role, while leaving other important characters almost entirely undeveloped, turns Fitzroy into the representative of a whole society, and Darwin into the brilliant opponent of that society.

Darwin, the viewer is forced to believe, almost singlehandedly brought an end to the world that produced Captain Fitzroy. This view is reinforced by the portrayal of the publication and reception of the *The Origin of Species* in 1859. The teleplay devotes little time—only a portion of one episode—to the depiction of the debate over the *The Origin of the Species.* To represent the controversy the directors chose the famous Huxley-Wilberforce debate, in which the social and religious consequences of natural selection were the focus of attention, and in which battle lines were clearly drawn between traditional religion and scientific materialism. In the debate scenes Darwin clearly emerges as the winner, and the viewer once again sees Darwin and his theories as the champions of modernism and the victors in a bitter battle against Victorianism.

Once again, written analyses of the nature of Victorianism and of the impact of Darwin's book are vastly different from the Time-Life version. Where the television play was in essence an attempt to recreate dramatically the physical and social world in which Darwin lived, Ruse and Himmelfarb, like other writers who have taken Darwin as their subject concentrate merely on a different aspect of that world—the scientific/philosophical activity that surrounded Darwin. Intellectual historians like Ruse and Himmelfarb view the nineteenth century as an age characterized by social inequity but also by political and religious advancement. Such writers, unlike the producers of the television series, stress social and intellectual developments like the expansion of the educational system and the abolition of religious tests—developments that rendered the scientific community quite independent of the social and political regulations of the time and made it possible for many people to adopt Darwin's evolutionist ideas with little hesitation. Thus, for Ruse, Himmelfarb, and other historians of the nineteenth century, Darwin was part of an important period of social, political, and intellectual advancement that began before the writing of his *Origin* and continued long after the publication of his last word on the subject of evolution.

The Time-Life dramatization offers a picture of the life and work of Charles Darwin that is significantly different from that accepted among historians. The difference between the two is not limited to a different interpretation of the life of Charles Darwin, however. Beneath the surface of the two works lies significantly different views of the nature of science and its role in society. The television drama gives its viewers a picture of science as a process dependent upon individual inspiration and coincidence and not at all upon the operation of the scientific community in particular or of society in general. Science and scientists, in fact, are pictured as the opponents and outcasts of society. Historians, by contrast, depict scientific discovery as a process involving many people and amounting, in the long run, to a very slow and gradual synthesis of ideas, which may be accelerated by certain people as it was by Darwin in the mid-nineteenth century, but which progresses outside such periods of rapid development. Historians' interpretations also dispute the television series' depiction of the role of science in the community. For Ruse and Himmelfarb, science does not exist outside society or in opposition to it. It is an integral part of the social and political community, dependent on social progress for its own advancement and in turn contributing its own accomplishments to social, political, and intellectual developments.

The contextual differences between printed and filmed interpretations are subtle, and might not be obvious to the casual viewer or even to the historian whose main concern is to detect errors in chronology, costuming, or location. Contextual interpretations and variations are present, however, and must be analyzed and evaluated as increasingly filmed history becomes a prominent element of the popular historical canon.

NOTES

[1]Robert Writer Reid, "The Voyage of Charles Darwin," *Time-Life* Television, 1980. Hereafter cited in the text as *VC*.

[2]Francis Darwin, ed., *The Autobiography of Charles Darwin and Selected Letters.*,1892 (New Yoir: Dover Publishers, 1958). Hereafter, *AC*.

[3]Gertrude Himmelfarb, *Darwin and the Darwinian Revolution* (New York: Anchor Books, 1962). Hereafter, *DD*.

[3]Michael Ruse, *The Darwinian Revolution: Science Red in Tooth and Claw* (Chicago: University of Chicago Press, 1979). Hereafter, *DR.*.

[4]Erasmus Darwin, *Zoonomia* Vol. 1 (NY: T. & J. Swords, 1796).

[5]Charles Lyell, *Principles of Geology* 2nd. ed. (London: John Murray, 1932-32).

[6]Charles Darwin, *The Origin of the Species* (London: John Murray, 1859).

4. SOUTH AFRICA FROM TEXT TO FILM: *CRY FREEDOM* AND *A DRY WHITE SEASON*

Victoria Carchidi

IN THE LATE 1980s, two "major motion pictures," as the saying goes, gave us cinematic treatments of South Africa. *Cry Freedom,* based on Donald Woods's autobiographical accounts of being enlightened by Steve Biko, and *A Dry White Season,* based on André Brink's novel of the same name, emerge from different genres, one explicitly fictional.[1] Yet each appends as code to the film a catalogue of death caused by apartheid, thereby adopting a time-honored method of attesting to a work's factual base—like the *Sound of Music*'s note telling us what became of the family Von Trapp. With these explicit claims, the films raise questions about the historical accuracy of these large-scale productions. Do these films use their genre's ability to represent real events—as in each movie's reenactment of the Soweto riots—to explore and inform the audience about the central issues of apartheid?[2] Or in moving from text to film does South Africa evanesce, leaving at each film's core a reflection instead of the audience's preconceived ideas? This paper argues the latter point.

In 1977 Steve Biko died while in police custody. The next year Donald Woods published his account of that death in *Biko*. In 1988 Richard Attenborough gave the world his treatment of that death in the movie *Cry Freedom*. That the movie has attracted attention in a way the death did not, leading to *Biko*'s republication in paperback, is not the result of happenstance. The decisions governing the transformation of South Africa generally, and Steve Biko particularly, in Woods's book[3] and Attenborough's film reveal a great deal both about the original source material and about our current society, although perhaps in ways not intended by either author or filmmaker.

Donald Woods wrote *Biko* under the shock of discovering the impact apartheid has on a white life. In *Cry Freedom* Biko tells Woods, "we [blacks] know how you [whites] live" by doing white people's chores, then asks, "Would you like to see how we live?" This line dramatizes the fact that every restriction on the black population involves a reciprocal restriction on whites. "Every person, black or white, has to live in an area designated as their 'own area.'"[4] But it is not until Woods experiences the restrictions he has denounced for years in his paper—till suddenly *he* is the banned person, suddenly *his* friends are arrested and die in detention, suddenly *his* children are subjected to unpredictable, irrational attacks, that—suddenly—South Africa becomes unbearable for him. This is not to minimize Woods's anguish over Biko's death or his anger at the South African government, but simply to illustrate how ingrained the patterns of thinking fostered by apartheid are. Although angry at the oppression of blacks before he met Biko, Woods nonetheless continued to live with the unexamined security of being white under a white government.

The strength of Woods's book is its immediacy. Begun while he was under banning orders, it reflects the pain of discovering one's loss of sovereignty over one's own life: Woods describes the dread created by the ever-present threat of police searches. Since blacks in South Africa must live every day with the fear that their lives may be violently disrupted at any moment without cause or warning, the book successfully conveys the oppressivity of the security forces, albeit not by direct representation of black conditions.

Its weaknesses stem from the same circumstances that make it worth reading: because of its passionate drive to testify against apartheid, the book is unwieldy, disorganized, and rambling. Writings by Nelson Mandela and Biko, banned in South Africa, are incorporated in undigested chunks, distorting any form the book might have had on its own: yet they also prove to be the most powerful and compelling indictments of apartheid, dispelling as they do any myth of black irrationality. Against the intense, articulate backdrop of philosophical debates and national priorities, the story of Woods pales into insignificance.

This, too, has been the major complaint with the film: that once Biko dies, Woods's story seems trivial. Yet the book draws strength from the format of Everyman—Woods—living and learning from the tumultuous events surrounding him; it manifests the human desire to illuminate the vast night of history with the pale beam of personal experience. In contrast, Cry Freedom cannot capture the sense Woods had that he was bearing witness, that his voice had to be heard because no one else could tell the story. The impulse behind a major film is completely opposite. Its urge is to tell a story that is spectacular, important, worthy of treatment on the Big Screen, and likely to draw big crowds. It is the end product of well-considered collaboration. As a forum for reaching the public, it is superior to a book; Attenborough states, "I wanted to reach people who were indifferent, who didn't know what was going on and didn't care."[5] His audience, then, had not been touched by the book, but would be by the film. Although commercial film—even Cry Freedom's three-and-a-half hours—cannot treat issues to the same extent as a text that can be picked up and put down at leisure, it does present events in a more visually realistic mode.[6] It must, therefore, sustain the scrutiny of those who have attended the films not out of ignorance.

There are several threads of representation entwined in the Cry Freedom projects: the first is Steve Biko's life, the second is Woods's book about Biko, and the reality that book creates, and the third is the film, to which Woods and his wife were advisors. Filmed in Zimbabwe, advised by someone not only exiled for a decade but with a vested interest in the version of reality he had published, *Cry Freedom* does not have an immediate connection to South Africa. Although it is remarkably faithful to Woods's version of South Africa, the film "is not a truthful one."[7] That it tries to be, however, cannot be denied. David Denby describes Richard Attenborough's attempt to find a proper actor—that is, one of the right age, height, and looks—to play Biko. He interviews Denzel Washington and likes him, but "there was one problem—the space between Biko's front teeth."[8] Luckily, Washington reveals that his teeth are capped, and gets the role. This same attention to veracity was not lavished equally on all aspects: posters in the movie's opening shots show Mandela's face, rather than the true heroes of the mid-1970s, such as Sobukwe (CD 42). Stanley Kauffman writes, "the need to stick to facts fractures the film cinematically."[9] The comment reflects the same error that caught Attenborough—equating Woods's accounts with the real thing.

Woods could not help but put his story into his description of Biko: their friendship fueled his desire to speak out, and was the source of his unique vision. However, for the screenplay to follow this decision and present Biko as merely a catalyst for Woods's flight renders the story trite. Critics complained that Denzel Washington's Biko had more charisma than Kevin Kline's Woods, just as in *Biko* the subject's voice compels attention not commanded by the author. Yet when Biko's testimony at the trial of Black Consciousness Supporters appears in the film, the situation is unclear; without outside knowledge, viewers would find the scenes hard to place with any certainty. And the sound bites chosen to represent Biko's thinking—that whites are more pink than white, for example[10]—while cute, do not reflect the depth and profundity of Biko's thoughts. One critic suggests that "the radical cutting edge of [Biko's] views has been dulled to make them more palatable to Attenborough's intended white audience of millions" (CD).

It is understandable that Woods would write his book for a primarily white audience. After all, he grew up in a society predicated on white dominance and power: that he would find it difficult to break those habits of thinking is excusable (and Woods does excuse himself [*BI* 42]). But the film duplicates these attitudes unquestioningly. Denby writes, "There's an element of priggish self-congratulation in the movie's warmth: Isn't this wonderful! An intelligent white man and an intelligent black man can get along beautifully!"[11] This sentiment echoes Woods's own astonished perception of his ability to accept the unusual: "Few white males in South Africa have met a [black woman like] Dr. Ramphele who could say quite casually, "Now you're really talking nonsense—here, let me get you another drink" (*BI* 68). The gender choices in these two examples introduce a subject treated below, yet note that Woods's vision of equality requires Ramphele to serve him a drink to soften her critique. The most looming flaw of the film is, as Denby writes, that Attenborough:

> wants to reach the mass of *white* viewers, and here his commercial and propagandistic ambitions become intertwined. The story of a white liberal's moral and physical journey is an adventure that ends happily. Donald Woods, Steve Biko's friend, becomes the lens through which we see South Africa. (OA 113)

Attenborough adopts Woods's reality, the film suggests, because he shares both Woods's mixed horror of apartheid and his paternalistic attitude toward blacks.[12]

A Dry White Season offers an interesting parallel to *Cry Freedom*. A pernicious—and not very covert—subtext of sexism plagues the novel by André Brink. The film, however, does not raise as strong questions about historicity, since its plot is drawn—and even then, rather loosely—from a fictional source. Yet this film, too, appends a hallmark of veracity at story's end, and the plot bears such striking similarities to the Biko story that the novel was banned in South Africa.

The differences from Woods's story inform Brink's own interests. Du Toit is an Afrikaner, rather than a "typical" British liberal. The subject of his investigation is a gardener killed in police custody, not an intellectual colleague, and Du Toit's concern at first is almost a matter of *noblesse oblige*—a suspicion that he gave the man bad advice. Finally, there is no happy escape from South Africa, though the film succumbs to a vision of poetic justice not available in the novel. In both film and novel, Du Toit is hit and killed by a car to silence him, but in the film his story is published by the papers; the novel leaves his material more ambiguously in the hands of a novelist—Brink, perhaps? These changes assure that Du Toit starts out as less of a hero than Woods does to those outside the Afrikaner community—and inside that community, they provide a dramatic conflict between true thinker and apostate. By raising the stakes, Brink increases both the potential impact of his novel and the difficulty of winning over his audience.

Further complicating Brink's task is the most radical difference between *Cry Freedom* and *A Dry White Season*—the role of women. *Cry Freedom* contains a number of powerful women: Woods's wife, Dr. Ramphele, Biko's wife. Even in her most critical scene, when Wendy Woods accuses her husband of using Biko's death for his own gain, the film gives credibility to her actions. In contrast, Brink's novel is riddled with incomprehensibly malicious and destructive women. As Du Toit pursues his labyrinthine investigation against the tide of his own upbringing, pressure from his employer, and mounting police harassment, his long-bitter, socially-disappointed wife takes the opportunity to berate him for ruining her dinner parties. His youngest, previously loving daughter deserts him at the behest of her dogmatic fiancé. His oldest daughter (a very bad mother to her children, we're told) sides with her mother against Du Toit. Only his young son is proud of his father and urges him to continue to search for the truth. Du Toit turns from his wife's hardheartedness to the arms of a young reporter, and extended descriptions of her body come to take on a far more central role in the novel than any investigation of apartheid. This seemingly blissful relationship, consummated only once, results in photographs of the liaison that lose Du Toit his wife and job and isolate him from his community. Interestingly, although his troublesomeness causes the pictures to be taken, it is the pictures, not his inquiry, that shatter his life. Even the one woman described as truly loving helps destroy Du Toit. Du Toit's wife leaves him, and his eldest daughter, seeming to repent of her former cruelty, offers tea and a sympathetic ear. Du Toit learns she is betraying him to the police, and just has time to get his documents to the narrator before he is killed. Although Du Toit's hit and run death is supposed to be at the hands of irate security police, by the time one finishes the novel one may wishfulfillingly read the murder as the act of an irate reader.

Clearly, sexism is not a problem unique to South Africa. But the virulence of its expression—every woman either has a full and generous mouth (*DW* 116) or wears a "dress designed for a much younger figure" (*DW* 255); we are treated to a "voluptuous nude blonde" inset in a car's steering knob (*DW* 79), and shown a cigarette lighter "in the shape of a naked girl emitting a flame from her vagina" (*DW* 148)—in a text ostensibly critiquing intolerance, illustrates the linkage of misogyny and bigotry in the habit of oppression.

The film of *A Dry White Season* cannot evade the misogyny of its source completely, but it tempers it. Du Toit has only one perfidious daughter, and she is given a hint of complex motivations for her more ambiguous betrayal. Du Toit's affair is deleted, as is the novelistic frame complete with its debauched drone of casual quickies. Even Susan, Du Toit's wife, is made more sympathetic as we see her change from happiness in the film's early scenes to vicious rage. At her most bitter, she remains a loving mother to her son, and with the brilliant casting of Jürgen Prochnow as Stolz the film focuses attention not on the novel's sex war but on apartheid. But even Prochnow's smilingly evil Stolz demonstrates a problem.

A Dry White Season has some strengths absent from *Cry Freedom:* in addition to having Marlon Brando to balance Denzel Washington, it has a lighting that reveals the beauty of South Africa (or, rather,

Zimbabwe), and it gives a fuller, grim view of a township, complete with piles of rubble, that nicely plays off the Du Toit family estate. But it shares, even more pronouncedly, *Cry Freedom*'s interest in the effects of apartheid on *whites* and its desire to find "easy truths" (OA 114) to the complicated problem of apartheid. There are two black victims in *A Dry White Season* to *Cry Freedom*'s one[13]: both Gordon Ngubene and his son Jonathan are killed by the police. But the film concentrates on Du Toit's discovery of apartheid's horrors, and the need for him to find an audience. What he is trying to make public, like Donald Woods, is that the police are responsible for the death. But Du Toit is more specific: he knows the death was caused specifically by Captain Stolz.

In Brink's novel Stolz functions as a representative of the security police's brutal policies: the film makes him their embodiment. This both creates a more dramatic opposition of good and evil between Du Toit and Stolz, and sabotages this film's own efforts to portray the intertwined allegiances that developed from apartheid. Localizing evilness in Stolz leads to the film's "happy" ending: Stanley—he who has initiated Du Toit into black life—shoots Stolz as he is packing his car, presumably to leave town and escape the publication of his misdeeds. Unfortunately, this solution is pure theater. Only through cinematic convention do we see Stolz torture Ngubene and run over Du Toit. When the camera freezes on Stanley in the instant before he shoots Stolz, and the torture and killing flashback, these are not memories Stanley can have in his head. One of the most painful aspects of *Biko* is that only Biko and those who caused or allowed the death know what happened. Biko cannot talk, and the others will not. That absolute impenetrability, the fact that all the fragments from witnesses can never tell the whole truth, is erased in *A Dry White Season*. Our relief at Stolz's death is unalloyed because we *see* him commit the crimes; there is no complication, no doubt. The movie compels us to want a resolution that plays right into the propaganda of apartheid: free the blacks, and they will slaughter all the whites on suspicion of abuse or complicity.

Notable as *Cry Freedom* is for its lack of gratuitous sexual innuendo and exploitation of women, it carries the stigma of sexism: the generic male pronoun predominates—Biko contrasts growing up in the township to life outside it, summing up, "no matter how smart or dumb a white child is, he has privileges." One might add, no matter how black or white a child is, *she* does not. A common argument against interfering in South African politics is the claim that blacks there have a better standard of living than blacks in other parts of Africa. This is a false comparison: their standards are sharply inequitable with white living standards in their own country. Beyond that barrier is that of sexual difference. Although a white girl will have more than a black girl, each has less than her male counterpart. This is demonstrated in a brief scene from the police attack on the Crossroads settlement during the film's credits: a young woman is pushed against a wall and her dress ripped off her breasts. By attributing the threat of rape to the "evil" police, the film has its cake and eats it too—the female audience is threatened, the male audience thrilled, all in a politically correct forum.

This criticism might seem overly fine, yet all decisions contain residual information. South Africa is distanced from us as it becomes text—as it can no longer be seen, its multiplicity of voices dwindle down to one. In *Biko*, Donald Woods speaks for the country, reflecting his personal anger and determination that economic sanctions, no matter how painful to the under class, will most quickly end apartheid and allow him to return to his house and Mercedes (Woods's lecture). Yet whispers interleaven Woods's own voice: some he allows to speak through his book, as that of Biko, the court system, and the police: others slip in marginally—the sounds of complicity, privilege, habitual oppression—and render the text richer than Woods himself intended. He is a better representative of South Africa than he realizes, and convincingly embodies the dangers of apartheid. A notice about *Cry Freedom* states that the movie's emphasis on a white family is "redressed" "by framing the Biko-Woods story with larger historical events"—the attack on the Crossroads township that opens the film and the brutal suppression of the Soweto riots that Woods recalls as he is flying out of South Africa. However, that context does not "redress the situation": instead, it extends the patriarchal tactics of the film. The film's choice to preserve Donald Woods as the central character discloses a belief that audiences will not identify with "Bantu" Steve Biko. Further, the decision to show examples of police force on a massive scale reflects a fear that Biko's death alone will not bother this same audience. Although framing Biko's death with the large-scale attacks—not chronologically accurate—may have been meant to show that the single death is part of a juggernaut, it actually works to play down the impact of the murder, as is shown by the number of commentators who effectively blame Biko for his death. Lally writes that Biko engaged in "dangerous" activities that "led inexorably to his death;" Richard Blake refers to "his suicidal rendezvous with fate," [14] and Stanley Kauffman complains:

> Biko dies too senselessly and too early. He virtually invites martyrdom by insisting on a trip to Johannesburg to address students. He uses no kind of evasive action, he simply dives right into a police checkpoint. He is arrested and beaten so badly that he soon dies (PP 26).

While many may agree with Kauffman, as I do, that Biko dies too early and too senselessly, some may have difficulty with the implication that Biko's death was his own fault. Such a surprising critique results from the elision of historical fact and cinematic structure. Kauffman later adds that Attenborough "had to find ways to beef up the account of a pitifully short life. The last hour of this film's 157 minutes is a mechanical thriller." Here again, the tone suggests that Biko's life was pitifully short because it cannot fill three hours on film. In fact, it could, had the movie been about Biko. But it is not, in more than the obvious ways. The film uses Biko's own metaphor of dinner guests—that blacks want to invite whites to sit at their tables, on their terms, rather than always accepting invitations to a condescending white table (BI 60). But every selection of the film makes clear that the only table that should be shown is a white one. Where Woods could not help including himself, the film *chooses* him as its hero.

In *Biko* the focus remains fixed on its subject, one of its most fascinating sections being the inquest into the cause of his death. Here South Africa is revealed through court records, in which facts and words change like quicksilver to reflect their user's face. For example, one reason police and doctors failed to recognize the severity of Biko's injuries was the almost magical power they ascribed to him: they thought that since he had once studied medicine he was capable of faking the symptoms of irreversible neurological damage (*BI* 318-20, 339). The film cannot linger on these aspects of the Biko story—the indeterminacy of what Biko actually experienced during August and September of 1977—out of fear of diluting its message that South Africa is evil. The stunning triviality of such a pat message is underscored by the irreverent comparison that kept creeping into my mind throughout Woods's thrilling escape to Lesotho—that this was a 1988 remake of *The Sound of Music*, complete with the family Von Trapp producing a prize-winning chorus, not of "Edelweiss," but of the African National Anthem. Film has a tradition it ignores at its own peril: in this instance the very simplification of the film's content belies the dangers of apartheid, and elides it almost comically with Julie Andrews.

Cry Freedom reenacts oppression as it sanitizes the blacks of the film—one (white) viewer exclaimed in frustration. "They're all so nice!"—the subtext reading, "if only the (black) people *I* knew were so sympathetic!" As Denby notes, "The blacks in Biko's circle . . . are so dignified in speech and bearing that they border on absurdity. They speak one at a time, never interrupting or overlapping."[13] Human tumult and anger are not allowed these characters. Nor is squalor. Although we're shown the destruction of a shantytown, the sheer horror of day-to-day life there is not depicted. Biko and Woods walk through a calm township at night seeming in total safety: everyone is wonderful, culminating in Biko, the familiar Denzel Washington. In contrast, the Afrikaners are big, beefy rednecks who laugh at Biko's death. Our expectations are never disturbed, we know who to be for without any doubt, and the movie works hard to ensure that identification with the oppressed blacks will be as easy as possible. One writer tactfully notes that "its emphasis on Woods may at least bring home to a white audience how forceful and pervasive is the suppression of dissent in that country."[14] The understanding is that like Woods, white audiences cannot really accept apartheid until it oppresses another white. Catering to such biases does not necessarily distort—Biko was a charismatic figure, Kruger did joke about his death, and apartheid is, today, widely accepted as morally repugnant. The film does the service of prettily presenting Woods's story. As Mark Gevisser memorably puts it, the film encourages the audience to escape Africa with Woods in his "Light Airplane of Political Awakening."[15] It provides no insight into the vexed political situation of South Africa, nor into the conditions under which most blacks live.

By giving us such a tidy picture of South Africa, both these films reflect less pleasantly on their audiences. As the movies try to soothe and pamper us they hold a glass up to our faces: their strategies illustrate the significant and seemingly increasing role oppression plays in our own societies. Woods relates that black groups were consulted during the filming of *Cry Freedom*, but they wanted the story told through white eyes, to convert white audiences.[16] The advice was followed perhaps too religiously—the paperback reprint of *Biko* contains photographs of Denzel Washington, rather than the actual pictures of Biko before and after his death printed in the 1977 edition. By playing to sexist prejudice, trying to allay bigoted reactions, the film demonstrates that its preferred audience embodies the values of a predominantly white, male, and middle class culture—the audience, admittedly, that holds the most power, and can most effectively change Western foreign policy toward South Africa.[17] But will that audience feel anything remains to be combatted after having its conscience purged, after feeling its own intolerances assuaged as if they were of a different ilk than the biases of South Africa?

Cry Freedom and *A Dry White Season* do not present the felt texture of South African life. Rather, through schematized representation of the extreme conditions in South Africa, the films effectively demonstrate that the habits of oppression underlying the South African Government remain in effect in the very countries that decry apartheid. Cicely Tyson writes: "*Cry Freedom* is the first movie that fully addresses the horrors of apartheid. Apartheid is not history. It is NOW."[18] These movies are also not history, despite their inspiration in history and their addends. Yet both movies do show that apartheid is, indeed, NOW—and, more significantly, HERE. Its unseen roots infect us all. As charity is reputed to do, the battle against oppression must begin at home.

NOTES

[1]See Donald Woods, *Biko* (New York: Henry Holt and Company, 1987); hereafter cited in the text as *BI*; and André Brink, *A Dry White Season* (New York: Penguin Books, 1979); hereafter cited in the text as *DW*.

[2]Clearly, some of these terms raise their own large philosophical questions, as "reality" does. Here I am relying on the simple observation that, "If the ideal of art is to create an illusion of reality, the motion picture made it possible to achieve this ideal in an unprecedented way," Gerald Mast and Marshall Cohen, eds., *Film Theory and Criticism* (Toronto: Oxford University Press, 1974) 1. These films could show their audiences South Africa in a way news censorship forbade.

[3]I limit my discussion to Woods's *Biko*, although *Asking for Trouble* was also used in the movie adaptation.

[4]Hilda Bernstein, *For Their Triumphs and For Their Tears: Women in Apartheid South Africa* (London: International Defense and Aid Fund for South Africa, 1985) 12.

[5]Chris Vieler-Porter, Interview with Richard Attenborough, *UNESCO Courier* (August 1989): 4.

[6]"(T)he novel is a linguistic medium, the film essentially visual," George Bluestone, *Novels into Film* (Berkeley: University of California Press, 1973) viii.

[7]M.P., "Cambridge Diarist: Black and White" review of *Cry Freedom*, *New Republic* 21 (December 1987): 42. Hereafter cited in the text as CD.

[8]David Denby, "Denzel Washington . . ." *New York* 21 (September 1987): 54. Hereafter cited in the text as DW.

[9]Stanley Kaufman, "The Past in the Present," review of *Cry Freedom*, *New Republic* 7 (December 1987): 26. Hereafter cited in the text as PP.

[10]*Biko*, 165.

[11]David Denby, "Out of Africa," review of *Cry Freedom*, *New York* 16 (November 1987): 114. Hereafter cited in the text as OA.

[12]For example, in assessing Denzel Washington's acting ability he says: "Nobody has really taken on Sidney Poitier's mantle yet, but I think Denzel can do it (DW 54)." A compliment, certainly—yet why must black actors be placed in a separate (but equal?) category?

[13]I refer here to characters developed and killed in the film. Both movies use the Soweto uprising to show that far more than the main subjects are hurt by apartheid.

[14]Richard H. Blake, "Nothing Personal," review of *Cry Freedom*, *America* 19 (December 1987): 406.

[15]Mark Gevisser, review of *Cry Freedom*, *Nation* 9 (January 1988): 31.

[16]Tyson quotes an ANC official's qualified approval of the film's approach, but M.P. informs us that the ANC was at odds with Black Consciousness, Biko's party.

[17]A point Attenborough makes explicit: "I wanted to reach an American audience because it was, I thought, in the United States that a

60

fundamental change in attitude towards the administration of South Africa was likely to be most influential" (4).

[18]Cicely Tyson, review of *Cry Freedom, Ebony* (December 1987): 66.

5. FILM AS HISTORICAL TEXT: *DANTON*

Elaine McAllister

IT IS A TRUISM THAT FILM, whether on television or videocassette or in the motion picture theatre, has replaced theatre and often the printed word as a medium for communicating information to the public. Film can influence public opinion, shape the popular imagination, and reach great numbers of people in a short period of time. The purpose of this paper is to examine one film as an historical text that offers an interpretation of events just as any printed text might do.

The film is *Danton,* a joint French-Polish production that centers around the conflict between Georges-Jacques Danton and Maximilien Robespierre at the height of the Terror during the French Revolution. The film was based on a play entitled *The Danton Case*, written in 1928 by the Polish playwright Stanislawa Przybyszewska. Although performed twice, in 1931 and 1933, before the author's death in 1935, the play found neither audience nor director until 1967, when Jerzy Krasowski staged it in the Teatr Polski in Wroclaw. However, when Andrzej Wajda presented his interpretation at the Powszechny Theatre in Warsaw in 1975, the play was, at last, fully appreciated. A subsequent Wajda production in Gdansk in 1980 led to the film version that constitutes the subject of this paper. The French screen writer Jean-Claude Carrière adapted it to the cinema. In so doing, he revised Przybyszewska's interpretation of events in favor of Danton, freely deleting references to Danton's suspected treason and corruption, and adding scenes unfavorable to Robespierre, such as the one in David's studio.[1]

As evidenced by the film background alone, a Danton-Robespierre opposition produced by the Terror has always offered a rich field of interpretation not only for historians but also for playwrights and filmmakers. The Terror remains an object of fascination in the popular mind, and, as the bloodthirsty fanatic, Robespierre symbolizes its excesses more than any other member of the Committee of Public Safety. This film, directed by Andrzej Wajda, attempts to go beyond the conventional stereotypes to question the Revolution and the nature of political power. To what extent does the film succeed? It attempts to look at the promises and disappointments of the Revolution and, in the exchanges between Robespierre and Danton, as well as in their public speeches, to examine the problem of idealism gone astray. In so doing it offers its own interpretation of the conflict between these two men, one that has occasioned considerable debate among historians and members of the French political establishment. In France it revived old political arguments between left, right, and center and revealed that, despite François Furet's assertion to the contrary, the French Revolution has not ended.[2] Its mythology is still powerful in the French Republic of the late twentieth century.

However, the first consideration is the film's retelling of the story of what happened in March and April of 1794 in France, and more precisely in the Paris governed by the Terror and the Revolutionary Tribunal. The film's first scene has no historical basis—a young woman is bathing her brother, a boy of six or seven, who is learning the Articles of the "Declaration of the Rights of Man and the Citizen" by heart. The scene then shifts to Danton's return to Paris from his country estate and offers the viewer a panorama of what the Revolution has become to many Frenchmen: the guillotine, bread lines, the revolutionary police, and the threat of arrest. The city is gray and damp and dreary. The citizens speculate about the reason for the shortages: Did the government deliberately bring about the shortages, or have the counterrevolutionaries provoked them in order to eventually incite a revolt by the people against the government? This scene contrasts vividly with the tumultuous welcome Danton receives once he is recognized by the crowd. No reference is made to the foreign or the civil war as a possible cause of the economic hardship.

Robespierre is introduced next, and the differences between the two men begin to emerge. Robespierre is in his lodgings; he is ill and has been bedridden. He is pale and slight in stature while Danton is large and robust. Héron, the Chief of the Secret Police, enters the room and reads part of an article from an opposition paper edited and largely authored by Camille Desmoulins, one of the outstanding propagandists of the Revolution. The piece is an ardent defense of freedom of the press and an attack on the Committee of Public Safety. Héron urges that the paper be suppressed, and Robespierre consents. This, although not the first historical inaccuracy, is more serious than some because it appears to be a deliberate distortion on the part of the filmmakers. Was Wajda willing to rewrite history in order to illustrate the evils of absolute rule? In any event, not only did Robespierre not order the suppression of the paper, but also one of the most remarkable things about the Revolutionary period, including the Terror, is the liberty allowed the press. Voices on both the left and right were free to print anything they pleased, whether factual or not. However, as a result of this episode and others in the film Robespierre begins to appear as an enemy of democracy and freedom of the press.

Despite the fact that his speeches advocate individual freedom and republican government, the impression of a dictatorial and inflexible Robespierre builds throughout the film and the visual imagery belies the man's words. In the introductory scene, Robespierre's next visitor

65

after Héron is Saint-Just, one of the most radical of the Jacobins. He enters and urges the arrest and execution of Danton. Robespierre disagrees, saying he desires "the triumph of the Revolution but not at any price" and then asks rhetorically, "What good is all the killing?"

Thus, in these opening scenes, the film introduces one of the central problems in the mythology of the Revolution associated with French political rhetoric and the historigraphy of the French Revolution: *les frères ennemis*, Robespierre and Danton. Alphonse Aulard, first professor of the history of the Revolution at the University of Paris (1891), enthroned Danton as a hero of the Revolution and the supreme expression of the republican and revolutionary ideal. His pupil, Albert Mathiez, challenged his master and enshrined Robespierre. Mathiez, a Marxist-Leninist, saw Robespierre as the ally of the common people, bent on leading France to social revolution.[3] The historians Georges Lefèbvre (a Marxist) and Albert Soboul (a Marxist-Communist) continued in the tradition of Mathiez such that, for the Socialist and intellectual left for the last seventy years, Robespierre has occupied the place of hero, not Danton. However, contemporary hiostoriography in France is dominated by the Annales School, which is centered in the École des Hautes Études en Sciences Sociales. François Furet, an Annalist and president of the school has "attacked the entire tradition from Mathiez to Lefebvre as a myth perpetrated in the cause of Stalinism" (*KL* 58) and "has attempted to rethink the Revolution as a struggle for the control of political discourse" (*KL* 51). The debate between Soboul and his adherents and Furet and his followers dominated the historiography of the 1970s and was temporarily revived with the release of this film. In a similar fashion, the film provoked violent reactions from the left, right, and center. *L'Humanité* and *Révolution* proclaimed it counter-revolutionary, and *La Revue du Cinéma* carried it as "La Nouvelle 'Affaire Danton.'"[4] President François Mitterand was displeased, considering it a distortion of the historical record.

Not only is the Danton-Robespierre opposition a problem for the historiography of the Revolution, it is also the central "problem" posed by the film in terms of its historical accuracy. The film tilts visibly in favor of the more earthy and human Danton. Robespierre is "the Incorruptible" in every way—he is coldly logical and calculating, the voice of reason yet one detached from humanity. His elegant attire reinforces the impression of aloofness and contrasts strongly with his austere living quarters and even more austere language. He meditates about the nature of political power, *la patrie,* justice, the role of the Revolutionary Tribunal, and the necessity to preserve the Revolution from its enemies both from within and without. Robespierre's words convey honesty and sincerity as well as inflexibility and even fanaticism. The words, however, are lost if the audience dwells too much on the scene as created by the camera. The camera distracts the viewer. For example, Robespierre must stand on his toes to speak to the Convention; the viewer sees the silk stockings, knee breeches, and elegant shoes of a short, wealthy man straining to be seen over the podium. This speech before the Convention and Robespierre's dinner meeting with Danton convey the impression that he is pedantic and small-minded as well as small in stature.

In contrast, Danton's open and friendly manner during this same dinner meeting tends to lessen the negative impact of his words when he tells Robespierre that "tout individu exceptionnel est supérieur à la masse." Danton goes on to emphasize his reason for returning to Paris: to end the Terror. He also tells his former colleague that the same men must not govern too long, that he, Robespierre, has no knowledge of the people despite his claims to the contrary, and that what the people want is bread and peace. He accuses Robespierre of not being a man. Danton ends by telling Robespierre that he prefers to be the victim rather than the executioner. Robespierre leaves—stiffly formal, dispassionate, and sober. Danton remains behind, very drunk, and tells Desmoulins and the others who have been eavesdropping on the conversation that he has Robespierre exactly where he wants him.[5]

Robespierre, on the other hand, has finally decided against Danton, The doubts he had expressed about Danton's honesty at an earlier meeting of the Committee, plus the failure of his personal appeal for unity at their dinner meeting, have convinced him that Danton is an enemy of the Revolution. That Danton's honesty was suspect was common knowledge even in 1794 and, although never emphasized, is referred to in the film.[6] Even Philippeaux, one of Danton's co-conspirators, tells Danton he doubts his honesty and is not entirely certain that Danton, when in power, will not abuse his authority. Danton replies that he is tired and merely wishes to end the Terror, because he was among those who began it, and afterward to return to private life.

The scene shifts to Robespierre. He has returned to the Committee after the dinner meeting with Danton, and he now calls for his rival's arrest. After some discussion the Committee votes to issue an arrest warrant that will include not only Danton but also Desmoulins, Philippeaux, and other Dantonists. The Committee members express some surprise when Desmoulins's name is added to the list and when Robespierre, despite his earlier defense of both Danton and Desmoulins, consents to the addition. In the film Desmoulins remains among the accused when he refuses Robespierre's later efforts to save him.[7]

The ensuing trial is the film's centerpiece. Danton refuses to be silent and challenges both the Convention and the Revolutionary Tribunal. He and his fellow prisoners know the trial is rigged and their fate certain. Fouquier-Tinville, the Revolutionary Tribunal's chief judge, is charged with securing their conviction. Danton shouts and rages before the crowd, becomes hoarse and refuses to be silenced. He says the people have only one enemy—their government. Eventually he realizes his words are in vain and that the people who so enthusiastically welcomed him on his return to Paris are unwilling to rise up and save him from the guillotine and put an end to the Terror.

The film ends as it began, with the spectre of the guillotine and a contrast between Robespierre and Danton. Danton mounts the scaffold and admonishes his executioner to show his head to the crowd. "It is worth seeing," he says. The knife falls and Danton dies; blood drips from the platform of the guillotine to the straw beneath; the sun is blinding as one looks up at the knife; Lucie Desmoulins turns and, staring blankly, ties a thin, red cord from her cloak around her neck.

The final scene returns to Robespierre's lodgings. He is ill and bedridden once again, sweating profusely. One senses it is the weight of his conscience as much as any physical infirmity. The young boy, neatly dressed, has learned his catechism and is reciting the Articles of the "Declaration of the Rights of Man and the Citizen." The irony of what has just transpired in contrast with the ideas expressed by this "Declaration of Rights" is inescapable. Robespierre and the Committee violated the most sacred tenets of the Revolution in the name of preserving the very Revolution that had established them.

For the thoughtful viewer the film poses a number of problems, not the least of which is that of historical accuracy. For the French viewer the problems are perhaps greater than for the foreign viewer because the film tampered with the prevailing mythology of the Revolution. However, with respect to the problem of historical accuracy, the reasonably well-informed viewer will notice a number of inaccuracies, even distortions. The most obvious distortion, or omission, is the absence of the crowd—the Paris mob. But do the distortions prevent the film from being considered history? Is the film merely another interpretation of the historical record? Or is it an allegory and not a historical film at all?

Danton has been interpreted by no less a scholar than François Furet as an anti-Stalinist tract, an allegory. The real subject of the film is Bolshevism; the Revolutionary Tribunal represents the Stalinist trials of the 1930s, and the Jacobin Committees of Public Safety and General Security are the communist parties. *Le Figaro* echoed Furet's interpretation when it maintained there was no such thing as a historical film: ". . . like it or not, a film is always rooted in the present" (NA 65). Furet, however, does concede that it is a film without a social context and without the people. The events have been reduced to a duel between opposing forces. But for him the film is still important as a polemic against authoritarian rule.

The screenwriter, Jean-Claude Carrière, also defended the film in *Le Figaro*. He stated that the fog surrounding what one might call "historical reality" was impenetrable. He and the director had, therefore, preferred "the dramatic reality" that was possible to create based upon the events. Wajda himself addressed the problem of historical veracity in an interview with *Télérama:* "Qui sait réellement ce qu'est la verité historique? Il y a polémique méme entre les historiens. . . . Un bon film historique doit révéler le psychisme des personnages de l'époque" (NA 66). In other words, the facts do not speak for themselves objectively and unequivocally. Their message is different for different people at different times and places. It is, according to the director and screenwriter, a matter of selecting and ordering those facts to convey ideas and information. However, for some, including the American historian Robert Darnton, this is not enough; the historical record still speaks clearly to the objective and careful reader. A historical film, to merit the term "historical," must do more than merely recreate an ambiance and give its viewers a glimpse into the period's way of thinking, its psychological underpinnings. It must faithfully narrate events since the facts remain important.

However, if one accepts Furet's notion of "history as discourse" and the Annales School's emphasis on *mentalités,* then the film succeeds. It is both Shakespearean tragedy and romantic drama, a meditation on power with death as the principal character (NA 66). Danton, the practical man, appeals to the people; Robespierre, the theorist, appeals to France and the abstract idea of the Republic. Both, to different degrees, realize their inability to control the Revolution's direction.[8]

On the other hand, if one believes that the filmmaker owes it to his audience to respect the historical record, the film does not succeed as well. Not only are there inaccuracies in historical detail but also important omissions. Scenes have been invented, such as the one when

Robespierre visits the painter David's studio, ostensibly to comment on the corrupting nature of power and the totalitarian government's penchant for rewriting history. If one searches for a balanced interpretation, then, in the words of *France-Soir,* the film is "a sad failure that makes one sad." *Le Quotidien de Paris* delivers an even harsher judgment: "It is guilty of the worst kind of theatricality" (EA 20).

However, as David Sterritt pointed out in the *Christian Science Monitor, Danton* is best if taken as "a meditation on politics and revolution."[9] In a sense this was also the intent of Przybyszewska's play. According to Daniel Gerould, she viewed 1794 through the experience of the Russian Revolution and the 1920s, and the play thus stands as a warning. Robespierre is the exceptional individual forced to assume dictatorial powers yet fully aware that by doing so he will destroy the Revolution he has helped bring about. He foresees that the Revolution will degenerate into various forms of terror and ultimately authoritarian rule, leaving behind its original ideals. For Przybyszewska such will also be the fate of the Soviet Union.[10] For many in 1983 the film was a commentary on contemporary Polish politics.

The film, like the play, does not explore the causes of revolutionary upheavals but looks at the forces set in motion by them. In fact, once begun, events seem to take on a life of their own. This was particularly true in France in 1793 and 1794 when the liberal and enlightened deputies who had brought about the Revolution began to lose the power to control and direct its course. The struggle between Danton and Robespierre is a struggle between opposing views of what needs to be done: to end or to continue the Terror. Danton believes enough is enough; he wants to retire. Robespierre still believes the threat of counterrevolution is strong enough to justify a continuation of the Terror. Yet, as the last scene of both the film and the play points out, even the purest of intentions and ideals can go astray. In defending the Revolution, the Committees of Public Safety and General Security violated the very principles upon which they and the Republic had been established. As the young boy recites the articles of the "Declaration

71

of the Rights of Man and the Citizen," it is evident that Robespierre is acutely aware of the contradictions; he knows that he has betrayed the ideal and abused his power. The Revolution has gone off course. In the end, the viewer is left with the question, "Does the end justify the means?" and in fact, is political violence ever justified? The film's answer is an emphatic No (FE 18).[11]

NOTES

[1]Przybyszewska herself was orignally influenced by Georg Buchner's *Dantons Tod*, written in 1836 and first staged in 1919. Yet she rejected his romantic and highly favorable portrayal of Danton in order to write what she considered both a modern and a historically accurate play. Her principle source thus became Alber Mathiez's *La Révolution française*, itself problematical due to the author's Robespierrist sympathies. These sympathies are mirrored in Przybyszewska's play, which tilts slightly in favor of "The Incorruptible" and focuses far more intently on the issue of Danton's dishonesty, both financial and political, than does the film. For a complete discussion of the playwright's life and work in English, see Jadwiga Kosicka and Daniel Gerould, *A Life of Solitude: Stanislawa Przybyszewska: A Biographical Study with Selected Letters* (Evanston, IL: Northwestern University Press, 1989), and Stanislawa Przybyszewska, *The Danton Case and Thermidor. Two Plays*, trans. Boleslaw Taborski (Evanston, IL: Northwestern University Press, 1989); hereafter cited in the text as *DC*.

[2]François Furet, *Penser la Révolution française* (Paris: Gallimard, 1978).

[3]Robert Darnton, *The Kiss of Lamourette: Reflections in Cultural History* (New York: W.W. Norton and Company, Inc., 1990) 46. Hereafter cited in the text as *KL*.

[4]Marcel Martin, "La nouvelle 'affaire Danton,'" review of *Danton*, a film directed by Andrzej Wajda, *La Revue du Cinéma* (April 1983): 65. Hereafter cited in the text as NA.

[5]For an early and favorable French language review of *Danton*, see Marcel Martin, "Danton. Les frères ennemis," *La Revue du Cinéma* (January 1983): 18-19. Hereafter cited in the text as FE.

[6]Albert Mathiez, in *Autour de Danton* (Paris: Payot, 1926), compiled the historical evidence to convict Danton and his associates on the charge of corruption and general dishonesty.

[7]See George Rudé, *Robespierre: Portrait of a Revolutionary Democrat* (New York: The Viking Press, 1975) 172–77.

[8]Marcel Martin, "Entretien avec Andrzej Wajda," *La Revue du Cinéma* (January 1983): 20. Hereafter cited in the text as EA.

[9]David Sterritt, "Danton," *The Christian Science Monitor* (6 October 1983): 29. Other English language reviews of the film, both favorable and unfavorable, include: Lenny Rubenstein in *Cineaste* 13 (1983): 36–37; Philip Strick, *Monthly Film Bulletin* (September 1983): 242–43; John Coleman, "Films: Head to Head," *The New Statesman* (16 September 1983): 28–29; David Denby, "Movies: Danton Lives," *New York* (10 October 1983): 87–89; Rex Reed, *The New York Post* (30 September 1983): 35; Gilbert Adair, *Sight and Sound* (Autumn 1983): 284; Vincent Canby, "Ah, Those French," *The New York Times* (28 September 1983): C19.

[10]Kevin Thomas, *The Danton Case and Thermidor. Two Plays*, 10–14. See especially Act V, Scene 5, which inspired the ending to the film with the juxtaposition of the "Declaration of the Rights of Man" and the exchange between Saint-Just and Robespierre.

[11]Also, Gideon Bachman, "Man of Heart: Andrzej Wajda," *Film Quarterly* (Fall 1982): 3; Kevin Thomas, *The Los Angeles Times* (14 October 1983): C2; Jack Kroll, *Newsweek* (10 October 1983): 94.

6. THE REIGNS OF POWER: FOUCAULT, FEMINISM, AND *DANGEROUS LIAISONS*

Majda K. Anderson

> Women have been the cause of great dissensions and much ruin to states, and have caused great damage to those who govern them.
>
> Machiavelli, *The Prince*

> If I want a man, I have him. If he wants to tell, he finds that he can't. That's the whole story.
>
> Marquise de Merteuil, *Dangerous Liaisons*

STEPHEN FREARS'S 1989 FILM, *Dangerous Liaisons*, can be seen as one of a recent spate of films that explore the warring relations between women and men. French theorist Michel Foucault's ideas concerning discourse and power seem especially suited to an investigation of this text. The film also offers an excellent opportunity to pursue issues of subjectivity, desire, and the formation of power relations in light of current feminist theory. According to Teresa de Lauretis, in her book *Alice Doesn't: Feminism, Semiotics, Cinema*, "Foucault's views appear most relevant to cinema, to its elaboration of genres and techniques, to the development of audiences through tactical distribution and exhibition, to the ideological effects it produces (or seeks to produce) in spectatorship."[1]

Based on *Les Liaisons Dangereuses*, Choderlos de Laclos's 1782 epistolary novel, the film *Dangerous Liaisons* examines the possibility of a woman with tremendous power and the results of her sometimes diabolical machinations. This principal character, the Marquise de Merteuil, uses her knowledge and power to make an absorbing game of life, regardless of the cost to those innocents involved. Some of these players are not as uninformed as others and not only realize, but relish their roles in her intrigues—notably the Vicomte de Valmont.

Both novel and film present a hedonistic aristocracy. The Marquise and the Vicomte use their superior knowledge, gained through questionable means, to manipulate those whom they want to control. As Foucault notes, "What characterizes the power [we] are analyzing is that it brings into play relations between individuals. . . . The term 'power' designates relationships between partners."[2]

In *Dangerous Liaisons*, the Marquise and the Vicomte's positions enable them to dominate and exploit not only the lower classes but also their peers, and it is precisely these societal and hierarchical structures that Foucault investigates in his own work. This film provides a useful model for investigating power structures that depend on knowledge derived from discourse.

Foucault finds exceptional merit in studies of power relations and concomitant structures of regulation. In examining insane asylums and other medically-oriented facilities for the isolation of societal deviants, he relates these historical arrangements with the development of today's stigmatized groups, particularly sexual "deviants" such as homosexuals. Feminists have found particular value in Foucault's work because of its relationship to the historical separation, domination, and subjugation of women in terms of power structures.

In studying the relations of power, Foucault realizes that power no longer comes from "above"—not from a monarch nor even from a benevolent patriarch named God. Rather, it is "equally, an immanent

76

process, tied closely to knowledge and discourse, which operates as a technique on all levels of society."[3] In their book on the work of Foucault, Charles Lemert and Garth Gillian further expound upon Foucault's expression of the seemingly obvious relationship between power, knowledge, and discourse when they rephrase "knowledge leads to power by way of language" (*ST* 20). Because power and knowledge rule and regulate, they cannot be divorced from each other, and without discourse in some form or another, there would be little knowledge.

Once sexuality and desire enter into the equation—"the desiring individual [is] both a product and producer of sexuality"—new forms of regulation are required and these again utilize the power/knowledge dyad (*ST* 6). Foucault recalls the efforts of the Church to regulate sexuality in the form of the confessional and the more recent attempts on the psychoanalyst's sofa.

> The nearly infinite task of telling—oneself and another, as often as possible, everything that might concern the interplay of innumerable pleasures, sensations, and thoughts which, through the body and soul, had some affinity with sex. This scheme for transforming sex into discourse had been devised long before in an ascetic and monastic setting. The seventeenth century made it into a rule for everyone.[4]

Much of Frears's film, as well as the entire body of de Laclos's novel, is composed of various confessions (and the telling does appear endless) in the form of letters and assorted bits of knowledge floating around, demanding attention and consideration of the potential power they impart. Indeed, the confessional becomes

> a ritual of discourse in which the speaking subject is also the subject of the statement; it is also a ritual that unfolds within a power relationship, for one does not confess without the presence of a partner who is not simply the interlocuter but the authority who requires the confession, prescribes and appreciates it, and intervenes in order to judge, punish, forgive, console, and reconcile . . . a ritual in which

77

> the expression alone, independently of its external conse-
> quences, produces intrinsic modifications in the person who
> articulates it: it exonerates, redeems, and purifies him; it
> unburdens him of his wrongs, liberates him, and promises
> him salvation. (*HS* 61-62)

The secret knowledge gained in confessional-type circumstances can be invaluable in power relations as well as for social regulation, especially to the individual who utilizes this information to maintain control. Both the Marquise and Valmont are experts at manipulating the various pieces of information they gather from young Cecile, Madame de Tourvel, the servants, and illicitly intercepted mail.

The philosophy of power and exercise of rule have been subjects of philosophical inquiry since Plato and Aristotle. In the fifteenth century Niccolo Machiavelli curried favor with the new Medici regime by composing his *Discourses* on monarchies, with exemplary historical references for both acquiring a kingdom (i.e., power) and retaining it. Yet power refers not only to national control, but also aptly describes the manipulation of personal spheres.

In his introduction to *The Prince*, noted scholar Max Lerner states that "men, whether in politics, in business, or in private life, do not act according to their professions of virtue; that leaders in every field seek power ruthlessly and hold on to it tenaciously; that deceit and ruthless-ness invariably crop up in every state."[5] No matter where power origi-nates, whether from secret knowledge or financial superiority, its appli-cation assumes the same position of dominance.

Between people in any sort of relationship, particularly an emo-tional one, power is constantly asserted and succumbed to—the roles of dominance and submission can be interchanged. This interplay allows for resistance on the part of the subjugated party and Foucault com-ments on the nature of resistance as an integral part of the workings of power. The existence of power relationships

> depends on a multiplicity of points of resistance: these play
> the role of adversary, target, support, or handle in power

relations. These points of resistance are present everywhere in the power network. Hence there is no single locus of great Refusal. . . . Instead there is a plurality of resistances. (*HS* 95-96)

When the power network is examined in terms of personal relationships the essence of Machiavelli's principles recur with the modification of Foucault's insights.

Dangerous Liaisons takes place in pre-revolutionary France, at a time when the ruling classes had reached new heights of corruption and indifference to any but their own elitist concerns. The Catholic clergy had only limited control over the aristocracy save by public denouncement. In many ways this period appears similar to the present—corporate profligacy runs rampant and Christian morals lose their validity when those who espouse them are discovered flagrantly flouting those very principles. Again, public exposure seems the only method of regulation.

The Church attempts to control as much public morality as it can through its influence in the educational system and by way of its substantial wealth. It plays a dominant role in establishing rules of acceptable behavior that the citizenry take care to imitate, externally if not fully in practice. Also to be considered are the fundamental religious threats of eternal damnation and the possibility of salvation. In the film, only Madame de Tourvel seems concerned with the state of her soul, and even she falls by the wayside when confronted with the insurmountable temptation of love. She goes through countless hours of self-torment, knowing that her desire will destroy her, yet she is unable to overcome the sexual attraction she feels for the Vicomte. She perceives the threat of God's wrath as more powerful than that of any mortal man (including her husband); thus, in this case, the strength of the Church does indeed seem mighty.

According to Foucault,

Western cultures generally consider sex to be a dangerous, destructive, negative force. Most Christian tradition, follow-

ing Paul, holds that sex in inherently sinful. It may be re-
deemed if performed within marriage for procreative purposes and if the pleasurable aspects are not enjoyed too
much.[6]

Obviously this is not the case for the illicit liaison proposed by
Valmont. Foucault would hesitate to refer to such permissive sexual
behavior as detrimental to the public. He describes sexual
"transgression" as something other than "sexual license" and feels "it
concerns knowledge and power, which are expressed in the conditions
of sexuality. Prohibition is the means of social power for controlling
knowledge and social action" (*ST* 26). Once again the Church and the
public eye make the rules and provide the surveillance to uphold them.
This follows Foucault's special interest in Jeremy Bentham's
"Panopticon" model for the eventual self-regulation of an entire society.

The courtyard model of the panopticon provides the surveillant
with complete observatory control of the cells surrounding its central
position:

> The architectural perfection is such that even if there is no
> guardian present, the power apparatus still operates effec-
> tively. The inmate cannot see whether or not the guardian is
> in the tower, so he must behave as if surveillance were per-
> petual and total.[7]

Thus the "prisoner" (wife, schoolboy, criminal, etc.) becomes his
or her own guardian, monitoring self-behavior as if constantly watched
by someone else. This, in fact, is what Madame de Tourvel attempts to
do when she tries to avoid an entanglement with the Vicomte, but her
"self-monitor" disappears just long enough to destroy her life (although
she appears to have had a good time prior to her ruin).

The Marquise and Valmont never have the worry of censure; they
are completely without morals and believe themselves immune to public criticism. Granted, the Vicomte's reputation leaves a considerable
amount to be desired, but the Marquise admits she works diligently at

maintaining her impeccable standing in the community. Valmont finds himself fascinated by her ability to do this and questions her methods, to which she replies, "Ought you not to have concluded that, since I was born to avenge my sex and to dominate yours, I must have created methods unknown to anybody but myself?"[8] Once again the Marquise utilizes secret knowledge to enhance her powerful position. Her philosophy sums up her opinions of the clergy and the power of the Church, along with disdain for her peers:

> Women, who, being truly superstitious, give the priest the respect and faith which is due only to the divinity. . . . [W]hat have I in common with these incautious women? When have you seen me depart from the rules I have prescribed for myself or lose my principles? I say principles and I say it advisedly; for they are not, like other women's principles, given at hazard, accepted without reflection and followed from habit; they are the result of my profound meditations; I created them and I can say that I am my own work. (*DL* 178)

Foucault "proposes that ethics should be grounded in resistance to whatever form totalitarian power might take, whether it stem from religion, science, or political oppression."[9] The Marquise is never content to follow the ethical or purely emotional pathways taken by her less adventurous or incautious equals. She is out to thwart the patriarchy in whatever form it takes, whether it be religious, political, or in family life. Her behaviors are motivated by an unadulterated pursuit of power. When explaining her past to Valmont she states, "I did not desire to enjoy, I wanted to know; my desire to learn suggested the means to me" (*DL* 179). Her desire motivates the pursuit of knowledge and power. In the film, she states her case to Valmont graphically:

> Women are obliged to be far more skillful than men. You can ruin our reputations with a few well-chosen words, so of course I had to invent not only myself, but ways of escape no one has ever thought of before. And, I've suc-

> ceeded because I've always known I was born to dominate
> your sex and avenge my own.

He finds her philosophy fascinating, providing he remains in her favor for information and entertainment. Valmont enjoys his own conquests but both the film and the novel lead up to the inevitable confrontation between the two conspirators once they realize they are no longer on the same side.

The Marquise appears to manipulate her key players with far more skill than Valmont primarily because it takes him longer to digest the fact that she is truly against him. He busies himself with the seduction of the virtuous Madame de Tourvel without perceiving that he has fallen in love with her. He amuses himself with the sexual tutelage of the young Cecile, creating an especially shameless courtesan. The Marquise eliminates one lover and takes another, making sure her choice will annoy Valmont in the process. Her moves seem far more calculated and less haphazard than the Vicomte's—his, after all, are motivated entirely by pleasure, not an unyeilding desire for power.

Valmont already maintains a high level of control simply by virtue of his gender. This remains the insurmountable obstacle to the Marquise's aspirations—there is no way she can become a man, so she makes do with those abilities she does have. As she tells her protege, Cecile,

> . . . provided you take a few elementary precautions, you
> can do it or not [have sex], with as many men as you like
> and as often as you like, in as many different ways as you
> like. Our sex has few enough advantages, you may as well
> make the best of those you have.

She appears to feel, as does anthropologist Gayle Rubin, that "sexual acts are burdened with an excess of significance" and should be enjoyed for the light pleasures they can provide (*PE* 279). Rubin's idea of "the modern ideology of sex" proclaims "that lust is the province of men, purity that of women" (*PE* 307). Obviously, in a society where both men and women enjoy lust equally, the significance of sexual acts for both is diminished. Yet, as long as the value commensurate with purity remains exorbitant there will always be a premium paid by women for maintaining their virtue at all costs.

Certainly Madame de Tourvel asserts the provincial notion that a woman's sexual allegiance belongs to her husband and that purity is indeed a valuable attribute. Even Cecile has heard rumors about the undesirability of a "loose" woman. She tells her boyfriend, Danceny, "if I am to believe what I have often been told, men do not love their wives so much when they have loved them too much before they were their wives" (*DL* 273). Indeed, in her article titled "The Matrix of War," Nancy Huston claims that

> contact with the male body is not a source of temporary infection or befuddlement; it is a source of permanent defeat, by virtue of the metaphor which likens the penis to a deadly weapon. Virginity is seen as an invisible armour, and the hymen as a shield designed to protect both the body and the soul of the young girl. Once she has succumbed to this first paradigmatic wound, all other wounds become possible.[10]

For Cecile, once Valmont has begun her "instruction" and overcome her virginity, her only decent escape from a very public scandal is directly into a convent. For her, there is no longer the protection of virtue, and her chances for a normal, reputable life and marriage have been ruined.

This conflict between virtue and irretrievable "vice" dominates the narrative in both the film version and the novel. However the central, and sadistic, controversy in *Dangerous Liaisons* relies on the demand, as Laura Mulvey puts it, for "a story . . . forcing a change in another person, a battle of will and strength, victory/defeat, all occurring in a linear time with a beginning and an end"—accurately describing the situation between the Marquise and the Vicomte (*AD* 103). The roots of their altercation can be traced to "desire," which characterizes not a "particular affective state or emotion, but [an] affective or social force, even when its manifestation is hostility or hatred or something less emotively charged, that shapes an important relationship."[11] The primary conflict is made all the more interesting because it occurs between two people of the opposite sex who battle it out on the same plane. The quest for pleasure remains an integral part of their struggle, enhancing the contest.

In the *History of Sexuality: Volume 1*, Foucault asserts that "pleasure and power do not cancel or turn back against one another; they seek out, overlap and reinforce one another. They are linked together by complex mechanisms and devices of excitation and incitement" (*HS* 48). Valmont finds Madame de Tourvel far more exciting given the virtuous hurdles he must overcome to reach his prize. Knowing the absolute power he will have over her fills him with exhilaration:

> Forgetting her duties and her virtue, sacrificing her reputa-
> tion and two years of modesty, to run after the happiness of
> pleasing me. . . . I shall do more, I shall abandon her, I shall
> have no successor. . . . She will have existed only for me
> and whether her course be more or less long, I alone shall
> have opened and closed the barrier. (*DL* 268)

The Vicomte thoroughly describes a situation where complete dominance exists, and without a trace of compassion.

Madame de Tourvel and Cecile become the obvious puppets in this play of power. Neither one asserts much control, nor does it appear they would even want to do so. Valmont repeatedly refers to Madame de Tourvel's "power" over him, but in actuality these references are simply reinforcements of his scheme to seduce her. When he says "the inconceivable power you have over me makes you the absolute mistress of my feelings," he alludes not to a potential dominance, but uses the phrase in an attempt to flatter her into considering his suit (*DL* 84).

Indeed, Valmont understands the deceptive nature of women's power better than perhaps the Marquise herself as he comments to her, "The illusory authority we appear to let women take is one of the snares they avoid with the most difficulty" (*DL* 92). The Marquise is better equiped than most women to avoid these standard pitfalls, as she already realizes the inherent deficiencies in the female position, yet she too allows herself to be destroyed—right after she convinces herself of her own invincibility.

Valmont warns the Marquise of her inevitable defeat after she admits to orchestrating his elimination of her rival, Madame de Tourvel. He apparently did not see, in the execution of that innocent woman, the true architect of the scheme. She informs him that

> when a woman strikes at another woman's heart, she rarely fails to find the sensitive place, and the wound is incurable. . . . When I guided your blows, I did not forget that this woman was my rival, that for a moment you had thought her preferable to me and, in short, that you had placed me beneath her. (*DL* 331)

In the film she informs the Vicomte that this, indeed, is her greatest victory over him.

Injured pride repeatedly provides the impetus for the dastardly actions of both the Marquise and the Vicomte. He finally wakes up and advises her to back down—"See then your power; but, take my advice, be content with having tested it and do not abuse it any longer. We both know each other, Marquise; that ought to be enough for you" (*DL* 343). This blatant threat, instead of striking fear into the heart of the Marquise, incites her to further test that very power, and she calmly (though obviously excited at the prospect of battle) declares "War!"

The inherent and prevalent prejudice in a patriarchal society against women acquiring too much power revels in the downfall of those who attempt to overstep the undeclared boundaries. Valmont seals the Marquise's fate by handing over her letters to Danceny once he has vouchsafed his own death. The only revenge he can put into effect before he dies guarantees that her power will be eliminated, and the evil she weaves will go no further. Foucault never overlooks that fact that "discourse can be both an instrument and an effect of power, but

85

also a hindrance, a stumbling-block, a point of resistance, and a starting point for an opposing strategy" (*HS* 100-101). The Vicomte himself is not without blame—he has created his own traps and victims. Yet, because he takes the noble way out by causing his own death, he will be forgiven by the same society that will demand the public "death" of the Marquise.

Frears leaves the fate of the Marquise inconclusive. It is painfully obvious that she will never again enjoy her hard-won immunity from conventional morality, but just what she will end up with is never made clear. Her panopticon-like death, a horrifyingly public display of censure, turns her into a humiliated and powerless shell of a human—her grave situation emphasized by the final scenes depicting the Marquise removing her make-up, knowing that any form of artifice at this point is futile. De Laclos makes her situation even more unpleasant in the novel. She loses a lawsuit brought against her by the children of her late husband, which leaves her virtually penniless; additionally, she succumbs to smallpox, which leaves her "horribly disfigured; and particularly by the loss of one eye . . . positively hideous" (*DL* 380).

The Marquise thus loses one of her key instruments in obtaining knowledge, another lesson to women to aspire to positions of power— she loses an eye and will subsequently be able to observe only half as much as before. This can also be viewed as a classic form of castration, with its roots in the Oedipal myth. Oedipus himself needed to lose his sight to gain the knowledge of his wrongdoing. The Bible also refers to the true price of revenge, "an eye for an eye." The message becomes painfully obvious; the reins of power are not for women.

As Foucault notes in the *History of Sexuality*,

> The Faustian pact . . . is now as follows: to exchange life in its entirety for sex itself, for the truth and the sovereignty of sex. Sex is worth dying for. When a long while ago the West discovered love, it bestowed on it a value high enough to make death acceptable; nowadays it is sex that claims this equivalence, the highest of all. (*HS* 156)

In a world threatened by AIDS, a deadly sexually transmitted disease, the bargain appears to be made with great frequency—sex does demand the highest price of all. For the characters of *Dangerous Liaisons*, the stakes are no less fatal.

NOTES

[1]Theresa de Lauretis, *Alice Doesn't: Feminism, Semiotics, Cinema* (Bloomington: Indiana University Press, 1984) 85. Hereafter cited in the text as *AD*.

[2]Michel Foucault, "The Subject and Power," from *Michel Foucault: Beyond Structuralism and Hermeneutics* by Hubert Dreyfus and Paul Rabinow (Chicago: University of Chicage Press, 1983) 425.

[3]Charles C. Lemert and Garth Gillan, *Michel Foucault: Social Theory and Transgression* (New York: Columbia University Press, 1982) 6. Hereafter cited in the text as *ST*.

[4]Michel Foucault, *History of Sexuality, Volume 1: An Introduction,* trans. Robert Hurley (New York: Vintage Books, 1980) 20. Hereafter cited in the text as *HS*.

[5]Niccolo Machiavelli, *The Prince and The Discourses,* trans. Luigi Ricci (New York: Random House, Inc., 1950) xliv.

[6]Gayle Rubin, "Thinking Sex: Notes for a Radical Theory of the Politics of Sexuality," *Pleasure and Danger: Exploring Female Sexuality,* Carole Vance, ed. (Boston: Routledge & Kegan Paul, 1985) 278. Hereafter cited in the text as *PE*.

[7]Paul Rabinow, ed., *The Foucault Reader* (New York: Pantheon Books, 1984) 19.

[8]Choderlos de Laclos, *Dangerous Liaisons,* trans. Richard Aldington (New York: NAL Penguin Inc., 1962) 177. Hereafter cited in the text as *DL*.

[9]Irene Diamond and Lee Quinby, eds., *Feminism & Foucault: Reflections on Resistance* (Boston: Northeastern University Press, 1988) xiii.

[10]Nancy Huston, "The Matrix of War: Mothers and Heroes," *The Female Body in Western Culture: Contemporary Perspectives,* Susan Rubin Suleiman, ed. (Cambridge: Harvard University Press, 1986) 129.

[11]Eve Kosofsky Sedgwick, *Between Men: English Literature and Male Homosocial Desire* (New York: Columbia University Press, 1985) 2.

7. THE SUBJECT IN/OF HISTORY: *HIROSHIMA MON AMOUR*

Nancy Lane

HIROSHIMA MON AMOUR BOTH IS and is not Marguerite Duras's film. She wrote the scenario—her first—in 1957. The script evolved in collaboration with the director, Alain Resnais, and the film itself is as much a product of Resnais's vision as of Duras's scenario. Her experience of making and seeing this film marked a significant turning point in her career, and not just in the obvious sense that she has gone on to make films herself. While the scenario and dialogues published in 1960 provide a coherent narrative recounting an integrated subject, the translation of Duras's scenario into Resnais's film produces a space—the gap between word and image—revealing a basic incommensurability between the self, the world, and discourse that drives Duras's subsequent experimentation.

In Duras's early works the conventions of traditional narrative remain largely unquestioned: *histoire* (both "history" and "story") appears to be something fixed in the past that preexists its telling, a whole constituted by a series of retrievable events, and the narrative (the telling of the story) is ordered and organized by an integrated subject that is "completely full, opaque and found."[1] The experimental style of the later works, however, undermines the concept of a stable, recoverable past and produces fissures in the subject, both narrating and narrated. The novels, stories, plays, and films that follow *Hiroshima* and *Moderato Cantabile* are increasingly characterized by those gaps, holes, and silences that problematize storytelling itself, and they exhibit a nearly obsessional desire to decenter both the act and the site of narration (just as the camera and the voiceover narration of *Hiroshima* do). In the articulation between word and image *Hiroshima mon amour* unveils the double writing the traditional narrative strives to close off and opens the way for Duras's later experiments in narrative practice, experiments that cross boundaries between film, theater, and novel. The film invites a double reading that will open a space to question the stability or even the possibility of *histoire,* both history and story.

Hiroshima mon amour is the first Durassian work where public (social, external, political) history appears in the foreground; up to that point the novels and stories are explored private (personal, internal, psychoanalytic) history. When the socio-political dimension appeared (the European colonial presence in Asia, as in *Barrage contre le Pacifique,* 1950, or *Des Journées entiéres dans les arbres,* 1954) it functioned in filigree in the background. The film itself lies at the intersection of these two axes; already inscribed in the title is a relationship of equivalence or even causality between a very public and a very private past. Read at the surface, Hiroshima (at once a specific geographical place, a cataclysmic event from the past, and a person—the Japanese lover) is the public axis that provides the site and the impetus for a psychoanalytic journey through which the French actress recovers her own past and reintegrates her shattered self. Typical of this sort of positive reading is that of Trista Selous:

> . . . the actress explores her own past and her own desires
> through the medium of her Japanese lover. . . . It is her suf-
> fering that is set up as a parallel to that of Hiroshima. . . .
> the actress retrieves her past, that is to say, there is some-
> thing fixed to retrieve and she recognizes it. She remembers

> through the Japanese man, but she carries out the recon-
> struction herself, and what she remembers are her old desire
> for the German soldier, her old suffering in Nevers, herself
> as a subject.[2]

The film does indeed elicit this reading, according to which the recognition of repetition leads to narrative and interpretive synthesis. The text's desire for closure is clear and ineradicable. Through a fortuitous conjunction of circumstances, the actress is led by and with her Japanese lover to remember, repeat, and work through the trauma of thirteen years earlier. The suffering and death caused by the atomic bomb and the young girl's own suffering and ritual death (she is entombed in the cellar) become metaphors for each other as parallels between present and past, public and private multiply at all levels. The relationship between public and private may take the form of chiasmus: The liberation of Nevers equaled public joy and freedom, private suffering and claustration (the young girl's grief and imprisonment in the cellar), while the public tragedy and horror of the bombing of Hiroshima coincides with the young girl's liberation from the tomb-like cellar and her escape to Paris. It is through journeying to the particular site of that public devastation that the actress will relive not only the pain but the intense pleasure of her awakening to passion associated with her dead German lover.

The actress's private passion and suffering are inextricably linked to the public horror of the Holocaust. Both lovers, past and present, fall under its sign, again in chiasmus (the German, associated by his nationality with the perpetrators of the Holocaust, is a victim who suffers and dies, while the Japanese native of Hiroshima escaped death there and survives to reawaken the actress's passion) and both affairs are marked as transgressions (public treason, private adultery). The German and Japanese lovers share that same quality of death in life that equates with devouring passion in the film. The refrain "You kill me, You give me pleasure"[3] that punctuates two of the actress's interior monologues is of central importance in the film, exemplifying what Julia Kristeva has described as "The implosion of love into death and death into love."[4] The Japanese lover is as alive as the German had been when he awakened the young girl to passion and is thus able to unleash that passion again. Yet he is also already a dead man; his name is Hiroshima. He moves into the dead German's place when he adopts the first person pronoun ("Am I dead when you are in the cellar?" (*HA* 87), so that she is addressing the dead German through him. This identification facilitates the transference of passion and suffering onto the Japanese lover, a transference effected by both image and text. Early in the film, for example, the image of the dying German lover's hand is superimposed on that of the sleeping Japanese man (already stretched out on the bed in a mortuary pose), and images of hands continue to play a large role in the film's vocabulary. Shots of the actress's fingers digging into Japanese flesh echo the day and night she spent lying on the dying German's body, tasting his blood; it was this taste that led her to savor the taste of her own bloody hands when entombed in the cellar.

Working at the visual level to link public and private suffering with passion are images of disfigurement, which stand in a constant metonymic relationship to sexual passion throughout the film: the opening shots of the lovers' entwined bodies are intercut with archival stills and films of the mutilated bodies of bombing victims; an actor in disfiguring makeup stands in front of the lovers at the parade, where large posters of victims of radiation poisoning pass near them as their passion rises. Like the victims of radiation poisoning in Hiroshima, the actress had lost her hair (hair is a sexually-charged element of the film's vocabulary), and the disfigurement she desires ("Devour me. Deform me so that I will be ugly" (*HA* 35); "Devour me. Deform me in your image so that no one else after you will ever be able to understand why our desire was so great" (*HA* 115) is a desire to repeat the disfigurement she had suffered as a consequence of her illicit affair with the German; the Japanese lover does on several occasions pull and distort her face.

Parallels in both word and image extend to the public and private geography of the two cities. Both cities are "made to the measure of love," says the actress. Images of the two rivers are constantly inter-cut—both of which are at once stationary and moving, recalling the principle of "movement that goes nowhere" that informs all of Duras's work. Both rivers are associated with death and with beauty. It was on the riverbank that the German soldier died, and the Ota waters carry death in the form of poisoned fish, yet the camera lovingly lingers on beautiful shots of both rivers. The personal geographies of the two places are also parallel: interiors (the hotel room, the cellar, the little shed where the young lovers met in Nevers) are the sites of sexual passion and tombs (sex and death are inseparable), while exterior shots are generally associated with movement: freedom or flight and pursuit.

A positive reading of the film implies a view of history (*histoire*), public and private, as narrative unity (*histoire*) and the possibility of an integrated subject. In a key image that opens the last part of the film, the actress addresses her dead German lover via her own reflection in the mirror: "I have told our story. You see, it was tellable" (*HA* 110). As Paul Ricoeur says in "On Interpretation," "Life is lived, history is recounted";[5] the actress's life remained unintelligible until it was emplotted and narrated.

Read positively, the act of narrating her past for the first time (she has never told this "story" to anyone—including herself—since narration is dialogic) has literally given back to the actress the voice that she lost in Nevers. The only sound from the past that is part of the sound-track is the inchoate cry of suffering of the young girl as she cries for her mother. The cry is translated into the context of the present in visual terms through a rapid cut from the moment in Nevers when the mother runs to embrace her suffering child to an image of the Japanese lover embracing the actress in a pose that is a visual echo of the maternal embrace.[6] Imprisoned for shouting her German lover's name aloud, she had become mute ("I finally stop saying it" [*HA* 95]). The mute suffering is given a voice in the act of narration; speaking her past leads her to repeat at the end of the film her lover's name—Hiroshima—uttering and exorcising her past love and suffering. Along with her voice she has recovered the body that had merged with and disappeared into the German's during the day and night she had spent lying on him: ". . . even at that moment, and even afterward, yes, even afterward, I can say that I couldn't find the slightest difference between that dead body and my own. . . . I could find only glaring similarities between that body and mine" (*HA* 100). As Kristeva puts it, her body had become a "crypt inhabited by a living corpse" (PS 143). Significantly, she has become an actress, always to be inhabited by "living corpses," always factitious. When she says to the Japanese man, "I've forgotten you already" (*HA* 124), she repeats the farewell she has said to her old lover via her own image in the mirror (*HA* 110). Paradoxically, she must recover the past before she can put it aside. By naming her lover Hiroshima she equates him with the city that will be doubly effaced— from her private life as it was from the public domain of history—once she leaves it behind, a departure that has been inscribed in the film from the outset by the train whistles and airplane engines that punctuate the sound track.

This speaking entails a new understanding—both self-understanding and intersubjective understanding—that she has achieved through now being able to read and recount her own past. As Ricoeur puts it, "From this intelligible character of the plot, it follows that the ability to follow a story constitutes a very sophisticated form of understanding" (OI 178). Her self-understanding must come via triangulation, refraction through the otherness of the Japanese lover, whose skin color is both like and unlike hers, whose language is at once like and unlike hers (grammatically impeccable, it is quite heavily accented). It is his desire—his gaze and his listening ear—that have elicited her story and constituted her as an object and a subject in the field of the Other. By placing herself there, she comes to understand and thus reintegrate herself as seen and as seer. As Selous reads it, she "recovers herself as a subject," and that subjectivity has emerged in the pull toward closure that narration implies.

At the beginning of the monologue cited above, the actress stares at her reflection in the mirror while we hear (in voice-over, signifying interior monologue), "We think we know. But, no. Never" (*HA* 109). Like the film's title, these words are ambiguous.[7] Clearly installed by the scenes that have gone before is a reading according to which the actress has finally arrived at knowledge, has discovered and recovered her past through recounting it. (In other words, "I thought I knew what had happened, but I didn't until now.") At the same time, however, the words deny the possibility of ever arriving at understanding. This phrase summarizes the unresolvable contradictions installed within those forces in the film that desire unity and closure. Such aporia work to undo both notions of "histoire" (history and story) and to deconstruct those oppositions (present v. past, public v. private, self v. other, etc.) that appear to structure the film.[8]

Duras has said that for her, memory and "histoire" are contained in places:

> For me, memory is something that is contained in all places and . . . that's how I perceive places. They contain history ["histoire"]? Yes, . . . I tell myself that places are what contain these memories.[9]

Identification of the past with a place is inscribed in the title of the film. Following the same principle of refraction through the other that allowed the actress to relive her passion for the German soldier through her Japanese lover, she seeks in Hiroshima the traces of a public past that will unlock her own past. This obsessive desire to find traces is evident in the first part of the film, where she insists on her four visits to the museum (*HA* 24). As the actress makes clear at the end of the opening sequence, her desire to know, to encompass Hiroshima is a scopic drive: "Why did you want to see everything in Hiroshima?" "Because, you see, I think you can learn how to really look at things" (*HA* 41). Seeing the place that carries the trace or mark of the past thus becomes equated with recovering the past.

Yet, as Ricoeur points out, the very notion of the trace contains a paradox. The trace is what is "left behind."

> On the one hand, the trace is visible here and now, as a vestige, a mark. On the other hand, there is a trace because 'earlier' a human being or an animal passed this way . . . the vestige or mark 'indicates' the pastness of the passage . . . without 'showing' or bringing to appearance 'what' passed this way. . . . The passage no longer is but the trace remains.[10]

But from the very outset the "Hiroshima" that appears in the film signifies "nothing." The horror of Hiroshima's destruction, like the horror of the Holocaust, renders both perception and representation inadequate, so that the traces the actress seeks are literally the traces of nothing. As Kristeva puts it so eloquently, "Our symbolic modes are emptied, petrified, nearly annihilated, as if they were overwhelmed or destroyed by an all too powerful force. At the edge of silence, the word *nothing* emerges, a prudish defense in the face of such incommensurable, internal and external, disorder. Never has a cataclysm been so apocalyptically exorbitant" (PS 139). (The suppression in the film of the image of the mushroom cloud that Duras originally called for in her scenario is revealing in this regard: it suggests that no image can encompass the "apocalyptically exorbitant" extent of devastation that lies at the center of the film.)

The illegibility of the traces of the past that the actress interrogates is exposed in the long opening sequence. The claims of the woman's voice to have seen everything at Hiroshima ("I saw everything"; "I invented nothing") are contradicted not only by the man's voice (with its Japanese accent) but also by the whole series of images on the screen. Shots of the museum and hospital in Hiroshima, newsreel footage of the bombing's aftermath, clinical looking shots of the deformed survivors and intrauterine victims, still photographs, recreations, and so forth are all twice-removed from the "real" and serve only to underline the unrepresentability of this horror. All of these images carry their own negation within them; they represent futile efforts to encompass or approximate the real, which is always only an unattainable limit, pushed to an extreme in the case of Hiroshima. In the sequence where the woman's voice claims to have seen the hospital, for example, the image on the screen is a slow tracking shot down a hospital corridor. As the camera moves into the wards probing the faces and bodies of the patients there, their faces are serene and expressionless. The camera's gaze slides off without being able to penetrate and find any kind of meaning. Their suffering is indecipherable; it offers no opening or foothold for the camera. As the Japanese lover repeatedly emphasizes, she has seen *nothing* in Hiroshima. It is not only the Hiroshima of the past that is unrecoverable and void, however; the present-day city depicted in the film is also "invented," factitious. As it appears in the exterior shots, it is a mausoleum, then a film set. It has been reinvented by its American conquerors, as indicated by the many English-language names ("Tea Room," "Atomic Tours")—one shot in particular shows a smiling Japanese guide describing all the "sights" to a busload of tourists. Even the language of the banners and posters protesting nuclear war is foreign—most banners are in French, some in English, only a few in Japanese.

Along with the impenetrability and facticity of what is seen, the film exposes the impossibility of sight itself. Evoking the moment of the bombing, the actress places herself at ground zero (Peace Square) ("I was hot in Peace Square. Ten thousand degrees . . ." [*HA* 25]), but no vision could survive the incandescent heat of the sun. The image on the screen that accompanies these words is an incinerated human skull that becomes the desolate expanse of ground zero, negating absolutely subject, verb, and object of "I saw everything." All of the images on the screen are visual correlatives of the scopic drive—not just the actress's, but that of the audience as well (the audience is *mise en abyme* in the shot of the tourist busses). The camera unveils to us our own morbid desire to see a horror that resists figuration.

The film problematizes the very distinction between private and public history around which it is structured. For Duras, it can be said that the concept of "le vécu" (the lived) replaces *histoire:* "this mass of unclassified, irrational lived experience is in a kind of primal disorder" (*LM* 99). This is what Ricoeur calls phenomenological, or lived time. The paradox of our personal past—lived time—is that it is inaccessible to us as such. It must be related to cosmic time—that is, it must be "datable"—before it can be recounted. Here is where history emerges; as Ricoeur says, history mediates between lived time and cosmic time (*TN* 99). The film sets up an equation for the actress whereby "le vécu" will be transformed into "histoire"—both "history" (the past) and "story" (narrative)—through her experience in Hiroshima. In the grammar of the film, she must arrive at her own past through seeking and knowing what happened at Hiroshima; her own suffering becomes intelligible to her as it is equated with the public suffering of the victims' bomb. It is narration ("You see, it was tellable") that has allowed the actress to construct and historicize her own life as one term of an equation wherein the other term is the bombing of Hiroshima. Yet the intentional structures of consciousness are swamped by the intensity of suffering on both sides of the equation: as Kristeva says, "the insistence on 'nothing to say' as the ultimate manifestation of pain lead[s] to a whiteness of meaning."[11] (That this suffering resists figuration is indicated by the suppression of the image of the mushroom cloud that was to open the film.) Just as the private past cannot be known without reference to a public past, however, the public past (or "history") is not knowable as such; it can be known only as a "lived past" through the private traces it leaves. Thus the distinction between public and private that allowed the actress to "date" (order) her life in relation to public events is undone on both sides.

Finally, the film resists closure at the level of the image, if not at the level of the word. Fragmentation and dispersion are established as the dominant mode from the opening shots, working against the pull toward narrative unity and problematizing narration itself. The actress's desire is to make occurrences—including this affair with the Japanese man—into events that would count as narrative. Her "story" culminates in the names the lovers give each other at the end—two place names that signify nothing, nowhere, and never. They symbolize a radical break in history, public and private, that is, in the end, not "tellable."

NOTES

[1] Marguerite Duras and Xavière Gauthier, *Les Parleuses* (Paris: Editions de Minuit, 1974) 17.

[2] Trista Selous, *The Other Woman: Feminism and Femininity in the Work of Marguerite Duras* (New Haven: Yale University Press, 1988) 167.

[3] All quotations from the film are from the scenario published as *Hiroshima mon amour: Scénario et dialogue* (Paris: Gallimard, 1960). All translations are my own unless otherwise indicated. Hereafter cited int the text as *HA*.

[4] Julia Kristeva, "The Pain of Sorrow in the Modern World: The Works of Marguerite Duras" trans. Katharine A. Jensen, *PMLA* 102 (1987):142. Hereafter cited in the text as PS.

[5] According to Ricoeur, "The plot mediates between the event and the story. This means that nothing is an event unless it contributes to the progress of the story. An event is not only an occurrence, something that happens, but a narrative component. [. . .] the plot is the intelligible unit that holds together circumstances." Paul Ricoeur, "On Interpretation," trans, Kathleen McLaughlin, ed. Alan Montefiore *Philosophy in France Today* (Cam: CUP, 1983) 178. Hereafter cited in the text as OI.

[6] The Japanese lover resurrects not only the dead German lover but also both of the dead actress' parents. In this scene, it is her mother and her loving, supportive embrace. His intense gaze echoes that of her fa-

ther, and she regresses to childhood under that gaze in the scene near the end when she is crouched

[7]See Kristeva on the ambiguity of the title: "Is this a love burdened by death or the love of death? Does love become impossible or is this a necrophiliac passion? Is my love a Hiroshima or do I love Hiroshima because its pain is my eros?" (PS 142).

[8]As Sharon Willis correctly observes, "If read in terms of the contradictions it elaborates, the text and the film of *Hiroshima mon amour* propose a critical reading of a theory of history as a series of monumental events which are thoroughly knowable, as well as to a theory of a unified subject for knowledge, for desire, and for history." Sharon Willis, *Marguerite Duras: Writing on the Body* (Chicago: University of Illinois Press, 1987) 34.

[9]Marguerite Duras and Xavière Gauthier, *Les Lieux de Marguerite Duras* (Paris: Editions de Minuit, 1974) 96. Hereafter cited in the text as *LM*.

[10]Paul Ricoeur, *Time and Narrative*, vol. 3, trans. Kathleen Blamey and David Pelllauer (Chicago: University of Chicago Press, 1988) 119. Hereafter cited in the text as *TN*.

[11]". . . the obsessive evocation of a 'nothing' that could sum up the malady of pain designate[s] a wreckage of words in the face of the unnamable affect. This silence, as I have said, recalls the 'nothing' that the Valerian eye saw in an incandescent oven at the heart of a monstrous disorder" (PS 151).

8. LACAN AND POSTMODERNISM IN RICHARD BRAUTIGAN'S *DREAMING OF BABYLON*

Mark Hedborn

AS LINDA HUTCHEON SAYS, postmodernism "gives equal value
. . . to that which is inward-directed and belongs to the world of art
(such as parody) and that which is outward-directed and belongs to the
'real life' (such as history)."[1] *Dreaming of Babylon* is a postmodern
novel. It is schizophrenic, a parody of itself, a pastiche tenuously glued
together by an ironic treatment of the detective novel genre, and its pattern clearly reflects the tension of Hutcheon's definition. Questions
raised by the text are the same ones running through the discourse on
what postmodernism is and on postmodernism's effects on art and notions of history. Specifically, what are the consequences of postmodernism if we posit that such a thing as the postmodern self exists? A
Lacanian reading of the postmodern elements of *Dreaming of Babylon*
seems to confirm through the allegory of a painfully fragmented self
that the postmodern self, although often schizophrenic in the way that
Fredric Jameson describes, is also potentially highly creative.[2]

Two key concepts used by Jameson to define the postmodern are
(1) "the transformation of reality into images," which, loosely trans-

lated, he equates with schizophrenia, and (2) "the fragmentation of time into a series of perpetual presents," which he equates with pastiche (PC 28). Let me clarify now how far I am willing to use and agree with Jameson's definition of pastiche.

Unlike Hutcheon, Jameson excludes parody from his definition of postmodernism, replacing it with pastiche. Where parody distorts a norm to create a comic commentary, pastiche is "a neutral mimicry, without parody's ulterior motive, without the satirical impulse, without laughter, without that still latent feeling that there exists something normal compared to which what is being imitated is rather comic" (PC 16). He uses *Star Wars* (1977) as an example of pastiche, or what he also calls the nostalgia mode:

> One of the most important cultural experiences of the gen-
> erations that grew up from the 1930s to the 1950s was the
> Saturday afternoon serial of the Buck Rogers-type alien vil-
> lains, true American heroes, heroines in distress, the death
> ray or the doomsday box, and the cliffhanger at the end
> whose miraculous resolution was to be witnessed next
> Saturday afternoon. (PC 19)

I might parenthetically add that this tradition survives today in re-runs. *Star Wars* is a nostalgia film in that it hearkens back to those se-rializations, bringing past into the present, and helping to fragment time, to take it from one place and put it into another. "We seem con-demned to seek the historical past through our own pop images and stereotypes about the past, which itself remains forever out of reach" (PC 20).

Let me offer a more current example of this fragmentation and stereotyping of the past on Video Hits One, a rock video channel simi-lar to Music Television (MTV). One very short segment called "Milestones" takes documentary news footage and inserts it between the music videos. Right after Madonna and right before Michael Jackson we see and hear John Kennedy exhorting us to "Ask not what your country can do for you, but what you can do for your country," or

Richard Nixon claiming that he is not a crook, along with the film of him leaving the White House just after his resignation. These clichéd "Milestones" are not put into context historically, are not framed by narrative. Far from creating context, the images that surround the clips drag them into the now. In a way, the segment becomes just another music video in a schizophrenic progression. History comes to mimic postmodern video and becomes pastiche. It becomes, as Ann Kaplan says of anything presented in the style of MTV, part of "the hypnotizing of the spectator into an exitless, schizophrenic stance by the unceasing image series."[3]

Pastiche is a useful defining aspect of one strain of postmodernism. It illuminates the "Milestones" segments beautifully. Still, I would prefer to include parody and humor in a more optimistic, flexible definition; otherwise, for instance, one would have to exclude from the postmodern a Michelle Shocked video that parodies the objectification of the female body in music videos.[4] The collage of images and camera angles presented, reflecting various video genres, is typically postmodern. The singer, in a tight outfit, dances in the foreground in a manner reminiscent of exercise videos. Behind her, in flashes, we see her class, men in bathing suits—shots of muscled flanks or close-ups of male buttocks. Throughout, it is a parody of music videos in general (though there are specific references to videos by Robert Palmer). The point being that although it is parody, it is also pastiche.

I am taking the time to map this out because *Dreaming of Babylon* fits the postmodern pattern so dramatically; furthermore, it can be read very compellingly in Lacanian terms. The two readings work together to illustrate the dichotomy of postmodernism—its simultaneous alienation and liberation of the artistic figure.

Clearly at one level the plot can be read as a simple parody of the detective novel or film of the 1940s. C. Card is the "traditional" down-on-his-luck private eye hired by a mysterious blonde and working in opposition to Sergeant Rink, a police detective. The story revolves around the mysterious killing of a nameless prostitute, and Card's im-

103

mediate goal is to steal the prostitute's body from the city morgue at the behest of his new employer. He manages to bribe his morgue-attendant friend Peg-leg for the body, then he hides it in his refrigerator at home. However, quite mysteriously, the blonde hires two gangs to also steal the body. Consequently, Card spends his time trying to outwit his competitors and figure out the motives of his employer. When he finally makes it to the rendezvous with the blonde, where he expects to receive his money and discover her motives, something goes wrong. He sees that Rink has handcuffed the blonde and is trying to get her to confess. Rink fails and, uncuffing his prisoner, walks off to have a beer with her. The end. Card's final words are "I was right back where I started, the only difference being that when I woke up this morning, I didn't have a dead body in the refrigerator."[5]

Obviously, this ending leaves many unanswered questions: Who is the dead prostitute? Who killed her? What was the motive? Why did the blonde want the body? Why hire three competing groups to steal it? Why did Rink suspect the blonde? What was his evidence? Why does the story have so many loose ends? Using the logic of parody, the ending might make sense. Most mystery readers expect the ends to be tied up. Doing just the opposite makes a humorous comment of the genre. Parody also seems to explain why C. Card wears only one sock, and why he spends half the novel just trying to acquire bullets for his gun. Parody can even offer an explanation, although a reductive one, for this text's oddity of oddities, Babylon—Card's powerful fantasy world, his realm of hallucinations—an ancient setting where he completely loses track of the real world, where he casts himself as hero in a conglomeration of pulp fiction roles. Babylon is the reason, simple parody would say, that C. Card is so unsuccessful and down on his luck; he simply daydreams too much.

What parody cannot explain is why Babylon is structured the way it is, something only postmodernism can explain. And parody cannot explain why the text dwells on the creative process used by Card to produce so many oddly interesting scenarios for Babylon. The book is as much about artistic creation as it is about the pathology of a psychotic character, something Lacanian reading offers as explanation for the excesses of the psychosis and its creativity.

Babylon and what goes on there are postmodern—a series of fragmentary pulp stories in which Card plays the hero, a world he scripts from films and comics, a world where he is always successful. C. Card dreams of Babylon, his imaginary world, at the most inopportune moments, but interestingly, Card's discourse on Babylon contains as much material on how he creates it as on how much he enjoys it. The chapter titles illustrate the various scenarios that run through Card's mind: "The 596 B.C. Baseball Season," "A Cowboy in Babylon," "Terry and the Pirates," "Ming the Merciless," "Drums of Fu Manchu," "Smith Smith versus the Shadow Robots," and "The Babylon-Orient Express." Card picks titles and bits of plot, villains and character names from the genre fiction he has seen, and then pastes them together in his imagination to create Babylon.

For example, the chapter called "Ming the Merciless" begins with Card, sitting on a park bench, as the postmodern artist:

> I decided to borrow Ming the Merciless from *Flash Gordon* to be the villain. . . . I had to change his name and alter his character slightly to fit my needs. That wouldn't be hard. Actually, it would be an immense amount of pleasure for me. I had spent a very pleasant part of eight years making up situations and characters in Babylon, unfortunately to the point of being a detriment to my real life, such as it was. (*DB* 62–63)

From "Terry and the Pirates":

> Sometimes I played around with the form of my adventures in Babylon. They would be done as books that I could see in my mind as I was reading, but most often they were done as movies, though once I did them as a play with me being a Babylonian Hamlet and Nana-Dirat being both Gertrude and Ophelia. . . . Someday I must return and pick it up

where I left off. . . . My *Hamlet* will have a happy ending. (*DB* 59)

In "Smith," Card brainstorms for his own character's name, eventually choosing Smith Smith:

I had used the name Ace Stag for my name in the detective novel about Babylon that I had just finished living, but I didn't like to use the same name for myself in my Babylonian adventures. I liked to change my name. . . . Smith . . . I ran some variations of Smith through my mind.

Errol Smith	Carter Smith
Cary Smith	Rex Smith
Humphrey Smith	Cody Smith
Wallace Smith	Flint Smith
Pancho Smith	Terry Smith
Lee Smith	Major Smith (I liked that
Morgan Smith	one a lot)
"Gunboat" Smith	"Oklahoma Jimmy" Smith
"Red" Smith	FDR Smith

There certainly are a lot of possibilities when you use the name Smith. (*DB* ?)

Babylon is also schizophrenically postmodern in that it pops up in fragments to suddenly immobilize Card, lifting him out of the real world. It is like Kaplan's hypnotic state. He will wake with a start to realize he has lost anywhere from a moment to hours of his life. He is trapped in his own progression of images, his private MTV.

Thus Babylon, or postmodernism, in this text exhibits excess as well as creative potential. This excessiveness is clearly explained by Lacanian psychology. Lacan maps the human psyche into three registers, the Imaginary, the Symbolic, and the Real. Through the interaction of these registers, one's self identity is formed. The Imaginary can be seen as a "realm of *images* in which we make identifications,"[6] and it is closely related to Lacan's famous mirror stage. The child is initially only vaguely aware of itself, but in the mirror stage it becomes aware of itself through a Gestalt image. This could be its own reflection in a mirror, or an awareness of its mother as itself, or an identification with another infant. "The ego, first glimpsed at the mirror stage, is the reified product of successive imaginary identifications and is cherished as the stable . . . seat of personal 'identity.'" However, there is no stable self; it is imaginary, "no *thing* at all" that "can be grasped only as a set of tensions, or mutations, or dialectical upheavals within a continuous, intentional, future-directed process."[7]

Clearly, Babylon, the postmodern, and Lacan's imagery register are similar. All three are fragmentary. All three are mutations, combinations of images. Babylon draws the other two together. Card uses postmodern art to create his illusory "stable . . . seat of personal identity" (*SS* 131). But why is he so extreme about it? Why does it act as a detriment to his life? Lacan would say that he has not been fully integrated into the Symbolic register.

Movement into the Symbolic register, that of language, law, culture, and familial relationships, occurs with the onset of the Oedipal conflict.[8] The child's illusory, stable, unified self constructed in relation to its desire for the mother is interrupted by the father. The desire is repressed and displaced; there is a lack, and it is in trying to fill this void that the self is constituted in the Symbolic register. "According to a successful Oedipal resolution each child will choose as love object a member of the opposite sex and identify with one of the same."[9]

A second type of initiation into the Symbolic, which helps create a "normal" personality, is the "Fort-Da" game that Sigmund Freud describes, where a child throws a toy with a string attached and pulls the toy back. When the toy is out of sight, the child cries "Da" (there), and when the toy is pulled into sight again, the child says "Fort" (here). This symbolizes the acquisition of language and its power to make invisible or absent objects present. "The sounds . . . replace the action and are then substituted for unattainable objects of desire."[10] "The symbol shows itself first of all as the killing of an object, and this death constitutes in the subject the externalization of his desire" (UL 512). This is the key to Card's psychosis. Just when he is being initiated into the symbolic register, something tragic, something he sometimes represses, happens. He is playing ball with his father, and as his father goes to retrieve the ball that Card has thrown (da), he is hit by a car and killed. What should be an event only in the Symbolic, the death of an object by its absence, becomes for Card an event in the Real. Jameson's rather oversimplified definition of the real is that "it is simply History itself."[11] It can also be described as that which can only be described from within language, for instance death, but which exists outside the system of language (UL 517–18).

This episode in Card's life propels him into the creative/torturing psychosis that drives the whole novel. As Lacan says:

> it is in an accident in this register [the Symbolic] and in what takes place in it, namely, the foreclosure of the Name-of-the-Father in the place of the Other, and in the failure of the paternal metaphor, that I designate the defect that gives psychosis its essential condition. . . .[12]

We can postulate that Card forecloses the Name-of-the-Father when his father dies. From that point on whenever he tries to enter fully into the Symbolic realm he cannot, because the Imaginary (Babylon) intrudes to ruin his opportunity. Here Bar expresses the pattern of the whole novel:

> What happens is that the subject, after his primal rejection of some important value, must thereafter constantly fight the symbolic or, as Lacan sometimes says, the Other and its intrusion. The subject continually has to make up for what he rejected, and he does this, since his three categories are disturbed, with a curious mixture of the three, namely, hallucinations. (UL 519)

Clearly Babylon represents the intrusion of the Imaginary into the Symbolic via hallucinations. Card's narcissistic success in Babylon is a series of repeated attempts to regain the illusory stable self constituted by the infant in the mirror stage.[13]

For Card the artist, this lack of continuity, this continual surfacing of fragmentary self images compels more creations and creativity; Card will go back and back to Babylon and keep trying to make up for the hole in the Symbolic. His lack, his desire, generates his creative material. As Lacan says of situations such as Card's, "For the novelist these situations are his true resource, namely, that which makes possible the emergence of 'depth psychology' . . . " (*ES* 217). Clearly the postmodern has a powerful role to play in Card's production. It has a less beneficent role in his personality, on the self presented in the text. Perhaps the more disturbing aspects of postmodernism are linked to pastiche in Jameson's more restrictive sense, in that they are more cut loose from a posited, stable, narrative history, more aware that the postmodern self is closer to the stream of unstable images that constitutes the Lacanian psychotic self. At the same time it is important to point out that Lacan would say that the search for a stable, unified self is always frustrated, even in people who are not psychotic. This potentially opens the "stable" postmodern self to the creative power of the images through which it constitutes itself.

NOTES

[1]Linda Hutcheon, *The Politics of Postmodernism* (New York: Routledge, 1989) 2.

[2]Fredric Jameson, "Postmodernism and Consumer Society," in *Postmodernism and its Discontents*, ed. E. Ann Kaplan (New York: Verso, 1988) 15. Hereafter cited in text as PC.

[3]E. Ann Kaplan, "Feminism/Oedipus/Postmodernism: The Case of MTV," in *Postmodernism and its Discontents*, 36.

[4]In this paper I am bracketing the feminist debate over Lacanian theory's positioning of women. Although there have been many valid critiques of Lacan on this point, feminists have also found his theories useful. The issue is too broad for me to cover here.

[5]Richard Brautigan, *Dreaming of Babylon* (New York: Delta, 1977) 220. Hereafter cited in the text as *DB*.

[6]Terry Eagleton, *Literary Theory: An Introduction* (Minneapolis: University of Minnesota Press, 1983) 165.

[7]Malcolm Bowie, "Jacques Lacan," *Structuralism and Since: From Levi Strauss to Derrida*, ed. John Sturrock (New York: Oxford University Press, 1986) 131. Hereafter cited in text as *SS*.

[8]Card has obviously entered the Symbolic to some extent, since he has acquired the use of language. The Symbolic is not limited to the linguistic realm, however, but also includes the subject's social relationships.

[9]Kate Linker, "Representaton and Sexuality," in *Art after Modernism: Rethinking Representation,* ed. Brian Wallis (New York: New Museum of Contemporary Art, 1984) 396.

[10]Eugen Bar, "Understanding Lacan," in *Psychoanalysis and Contemporary Science*, vol. 3, eds. Leo Goldberger and Victor H. Rosen (New York: International Universities Press, 1974) 511. Hereafter cited in text as UL.

[11]Jameson, "Imaginary and Symbolic in Lacan: Marxism, Psychoanalytic Criticism, and the Problem of the Subject," *New Left Review* 55-56 (1977): 384. Hereafter cited as IS.

[12]Jacques Lacan, *Ecrits: A Selection*, trans. Alan Sheridan (New York: Norton, 1977) 213. Hereafter cited in text as ES.

[13]Jameson calls the "Deleuze-Guattari celebration of schizophrenia" . . . "the palpable impossibility of returning to an archaic, pre-verbal [imaginary] stage of the psyche" (IS 359). C. Card appears to be at least partially guilty of this charge.

9. DIALECTIC OF TRANSVALUATION IN EDITH WHARTON'S *THE HOUSE OF MIRTH*

Rita di Giuseppe

EDITH WHARTON (1862-1937) WAS INSTALLED relatively late in the American republic of letters. Notwithstanding the enormous popular success of her novels, early scholars of her work clung hard and fast to the belief that "one cannot be an artist and a lady," and Ludwig Lewishon, who pronounced this verdict in 1932, enjoyed a substantial critical following for a number of decades to come.[1] It was not until the mid-sixties that serious recognition of this writer began, and in one of the first biographies to take into account both the woman and the artist, Grace Kellog establishes Edith Wharton "as the first realist in American fiction and as the sole historian of an American social epoch which has vanished forever in the mists of the past."[2] With *The House of Mirth* (1905) Wharton takes the measure of the country at the turn of the century, and in so doing offers an altogether new version of the relationship between consciousness and society.[3] Her stance is one of skepticism and irony in viewing the actual economic base of American society, of sounding out the real and metaphorical relation between inherited wealth and commerce and the way in which any individual's destiny is determined by these forces at work in society.

The word "society" raises all the problems of the territorial boundary separating "art" from "reality." The complex transactions existing between "literature" (either the single text, or the entire corpus) and "society" (which can be a particular community or the large-scale social metastructure) represent a critical crux which will continue to fascinate us as long as the two exist. Critics from Plato and Aristotle on have known that literature is essentially "social"—having social causes, contents, and effects. The question is how valuable this insight is in terms of literary criticism. I would like to suggest that Wharton in *The House of Mirth* takes a view of society which is simultaneously the "society" created within the work and the "society" in which the work is created, which makes it difficult to examine this novel solely through autotelic theories of literature, that is, theories that assume literary works to be self-sustaining, coherent structures. Rather, any reading of it must rely also on the insights available to the critic in the application of historicist theories of literature that set the literary work in the context of the ideas, conventions, and attitudes of the period in which it was written. If it is impossible to deny that Wharton's fictions are "novels of manners," it is less difficult today to see that her scope goes beyond the limitations of this label. A case in point is M. M. Bakhtin's observations concerning what he classifies as the most significant type of novel of emergence, or *Bildungsroman*.

> In it man's individual emergence is inseparably linked to historical emergence. . . . He is no longer within an epoch, but on the border between two epochs, at the transition point from one to the other. This transition is accomplished in him and through him.[4]

In perhaps no other novel of its epoch is the love-hate relationship with America's genteel tradition more poignantly displayed than in *The House of Mirth*. In it, Wharton demonstrates her acute perception of the complex and subtle interplay between personal destinies and the destiny foreordained by one's particular social situation. Diana Trilling, in a perceptive 1947 essay, sees Wharton's novel as a sort of prototype of the Marxian protest literature of the 'thirties, but for reasons that would have been unacceptable in Wharton's day and may still be offensive to some today.

> Fortified as she was in her own class, she knew the reality
> of class as no theoretical Marxist or social egalitarian can
> know it: not speculatively but in her bones.[5]

In her minute descriptions of the social conventions of the late nineteenth century, Wharton in truth lays bare the ambiguity at the very heart of these conventions, which are regarded on one hand as the blunt instrument of a privileged class wielded toward maintenance of a status quo, and on the other as experience accumulated in time, that is to say, as the raw material of history itself.

Observed through the lens, say, of the behaviorist, the heroine of her novel, Lily Bart, in her journey from innocence to experience, appears to respond to conflicting values, acting and reacting to two codes of behavior which are at cross purposes. But Wharton's novel goes well beyond the scope of the "novel of manners" simply because it is not limited to observations of behavior; indeed, it is a piece of social reporting that documents the prevaricating nature of some of the philosophic and socioeconomic principles implicit in the culture of her day. In philosophical terms she represents the dialectic between determinism and free will, and in socio-economic terms between use value and exchange value. The result is a novel of ironic reversals where the heroine, through rapidly succeeding events, is transformed from the apple of fate's eye to a pawn in the game of New York's socialites (in which every concession has its recognized quid pro quo) to, ultimately, the proverbial fly to wanton gods.

Faced with the dilemma of choosing an identity for herself, Lily Bart (whose name transparently symbolizes the bartering of innocence) adheres almost unconsciously, as though by conditioned reflex, to the rules of exchange value in offering herself as merchandise for a prospective wealthy husband. But in a society of perpetual adjustment, where the terms of exchange are constantly shifting, the heroine intuits that the principles that determine merit and importance of the individual are so unstable as to tempt her to leave the mental enclosures of the aristocratic society she inhabits and venture into a new realm of values—that of satisfying her need for love—for which she soon discovers she is ill-equipped. The origin of the title of the novel sheds much light on Lily's dilemma, which concerns the nature of wisdom: "Sorrow is better than laughter for by sadness of countenance the heart is made better. The heart of the wise is in the house of mourning, but the heart of fools is in the house of mirth" (Ecclesiastes 7:5). Wharton's indictment, that financial and emotional security do not come in the same package, is a fairly trite premise even for the turn-of-the-century New York she depicts in her novel—or would be, were it not for the fact that something more than "you cannot have your cake and eat it" is at work here.

Whether approached philosophically or sociologically, *The House of Mirth* depicts two opposing world views: that of the libertarians who believe in the principle of free will, and whose conviction it is that individuals can and must create themselves by choosing freely; and that of the determinists, who ascribe concrete and precise values to reality. In that world not only are people determined and even created by social conditioning, but their relationships, personalities, and moral lives are simply illustrative of the classes to which they belong. Many philosophers have attempted to reconcile or at least to soften the contrast between determinism and freedom, and Immanuel Kant's metaphysical proposal is one of the most important contributions in this direction. According to Kant, everyone belongs both to the phenomenal (scientific) order, where one is determined, and the noumenal (moral) order, where one is free. For non-metaphysical philosophers, the controversy is meaningless because it is unresolvable. Still others offer linguistic and conceptual analyses to reconcile the controversy. Of the American philosophers, William James can be said to have dedicated his life's work to "the dilemma of determinism" and "whereas Kant argued that certain principles constituted our knowledge and regulated our activity," James held "with Renouvier and against Kant, that all ultimate principles were regulative, postulated, acts of will."[6] Edith Wharton seems to follow a similar logic in her novel, that both freedom and determinism are postulates of rules of procedure, and if considered in terms of degree, determinism and indeterminism ultimately depend on how few and how simple one considers the laws of our world to be.

However we judge Wharton as a philosopher, there is no doubt that the life of her heroine is governed by chance, the nature of which is very similar to James's tychism, a theory that holds chance to be an objective reality at work in the universe. Of importance now, however, is the need to recognize that *The House of Mirth,* as a novel about double standards, represents to a larger degree than it is given credit the same dual principle at the heart of the American novel in general. It has been argued that the duality of the American novel is the result of a double tradition in its history, which can be summarized in terms of two distinct strains, a native inheritance and the cosmopolitan tradition—or, to word this differently, of the self and society. If one of the great problems afflicting the modern novel has been to distinguish between the self and society, but at the same time to find a strong enough structure to represent them together, then one can venture to say that *The House of Mirth* has achieved this ambitious goal. As eyewitness to the shift in values taking place at the turn of the century, the author subtly weaves together threads of genteel tradition and human endeavor, recomposing the fast-fading links between the "gilded age" of the colonial mansion and the "chrome age" of the skyscraper. In the words of George Santayana,

> the American Will inhabits the skyscraper; the American Intellect inhabits the colonial mansion. The one is the sphere of the American man; the other, at least predominantly, of the American woman. The one is all aggressive enterprise; the other is all genteel tradition.[7]

In *The House of Mirth* the author depicts a situation that leaves little space to matters of the spirit in the management of everyday life, to the extent that her characters speak of their intimate selves in dialogues that would not be out of place in the mouths of today's financial gurus talking about the stock market. The manners she describes are those of a social class grown complacent in its assurance of inherited wealth and position, and rigid in its refusal to recognize the new forces and changed values already present. A typical example of the immovable aristocrat is Lily's aunt, Mrs. Peniston: "To attempt to bring her into active relation with life was like tugging at a piece of furniture which has been screwed to the floor" (*HM* 44). In subsequent novels, and in *The Age of Innocence* (1920), Wharton is less humorous in her reference to "the way of people who dreaded scandal more than disease, who placed decency above courage, and who considered that nothing was more ill-bred than 'scenes' except the behaviour of those who gave rise to them."[8]

The House of Mirth focuses on the precise moment in history when America was preparing for democratic integration and mobility between classes, when the Fifth Avenue gentleman was being pushed unceremoniously aside to make room for a new elite in the persons of the Wall Street businessman and the New York lawyer. It was also a moment in history when a beautiful, well-bred but unmoneyed woman was expected to show gratitude for financial assistance with something slightly more concrete than witty conversation—in literature as well as in life. As a woman and an aristocrat, Wharton enjoyed a unique point of view for her narrative; indeed, what most offended contemporary readers was that its author was at once member and critic of the social group whose vicious hypocrisies she unmasked. Therein lies her strength; her attack was within the family.

Concentrating as it does on the relation between social realities and the life of the emotions, it is almost certain that *The House of Mirth* was conceived in the light of some of the theories of America's first psychologist, William James—theories no doubt familiar to Wharton. First published in 1890, *The Principles of Psychology* was an immediate success both as a literary and as a scientific work. The chapter "Habit" became a classic; it emphasized the importance of "first experience," which establishes a neural path for future experiences: it is essential to establish desirable neural paths, argued James, to make our nervous system our ally and not our enemy.

In the case of Wharton's heroine, Lily Bart, the broad outlines of her upbringing were determined by conventions of the period and the class to which she was born, but to which, strictly speaking, she no longer belongs. Following James, the reader can observe how Wharton traces the "neural path" of her heroine's first experiences of wealth and security (up to her coming-out party), only to place it in sharp contrast with her subsequent experiences of poverty and the status of orphan (through the bankruptcy of her father and the death of both her parents). She depends, for her social status, on the kindness of friends, on invitations to their social gatherings, and on the charity of a wealthy and bigoted aunt with whom she lives. Her unorthodox condition places her automatically on the fringes of the social class to which she was born, where she is made to measure herself against other members of this fringe. In other words, as *nouveau pauvre* Lily can compete neither with her class of origin nor with the *nouveaux riches* of New York. The situation of the novel, then, is that of a heroine who becomes a sort of pariah within her class of origin because she has no money, and a very interesting prey to the new class because she has both breeding and beauty. If mismanaged, however, these assets run the risk of becoming liabilities.

> Lily understood that beauty is only the raw material of conquest, and that to convert it into success other arts are required. She knew that to betray any sense of superiority was a subtler form of the stupidity her mother denounced, and it did not take her long to learn that a beauty needs more tact than the possessor of an average set of features. (*HM* 40)

All this is summoned to mind by the heroine in the early chapters of the novel which, in fact, begins *in medias res* with Lily at twenty-nine years of age and waking to the fact that her survival (a word repeated throughout the novel) depends on her ability to attract and snare a wealthy husband. The reader is immediately made aware that Lily possesses by birthright a desirable neural path (or first experience) that she is no longer capable of sustaining, and she is faced instead with an impossible alternative—poverty and insecurity. The result, to use William James's expression, is that her nervous system becomes her enemy and not her ally. In the course of the novel Wharton focuses on her heroine's dawning self-awareness, which culminates at the close of the story only to give way to a tragic sequence of events.

> Her whole past was re-enacting itself at a hundred diffferent points of consciousness. Where was the drug that could still this legion of insurgent nerves? . . . the action of the drug was incalculable, and the addition of a few drops to the regular dose would probably do no more than procure for her the rest she so desperately needed. . . . She did not, in truth, consider the question very closely . . . darkness, darkness was what she must have at any cost. (*HM* 343)

Lily dies by a self-administered overdose (made accidental through sheer ignorance) of chloral hydrate, the fashionable sedative and hypnotic of her day.

One of the basic tenets of James's psychology, and of his pragmatic philosophy, an idea which draws on Charles Darwin's theory, is that in the course of evolution the mind has come to operate through nerves and brain cells so as to enable the whole organism to adapt to its environment and survive. Wharton apparently appropriates this and other ideas of popular Darwinism by suggesting that Lily could not adapt (she refuses a proposal of marriage from the detestable Rosedale, the fictional stereotype of an unattractive, upwardly mobile Jew who can give Lily undreamed-of wealth in exchange for her pedigree). And it is with the figure of Rosedale that Wharton enters the arena of the determinist/free will debate.

On close inspection, the reader begins to understand that the stereotyping of Rosedale is not the result of a lapse in style, but rather that it possesses a specific and important narrative function. The principal plea for free will is that unless there is a real choice, so that one can act differently in identical circumstances, there can be no moral responsibility. James, in "The Dilemma of Determinism," perhaps uncertain that he has made his point, adds a lengthy footnote of which the essence is, "'Free-will' does not say that everything that is physically conceivable is also morally possible. It merely says that of alternatives that really *tempt* our will more than one is really possible."[9] It would appear, then, that Wharton was precluding real choices for Lily in order to put aside the question of moral responsibility of her death. She saw to this by personifying exchange value—a principle that Lily not only knows by heart but that governs her every action—through short, fat, and wealthy Rosedale, toward whom Lily feels repulsion, juxtaposed with the personification of use value in the guise of tall, dark, handsome, and poor Selden, whom Lily loves and from whom she awaits some sort of sign that her love is not unrequited.

It should be mentioned here that, as a lawyer, Lawrence Selden has to work for a living and in the eyes of the society of the novel he is "poor," and therefore one of the members of the fringe. He is a man of potential quality, however, in that he enjoys his work, is sensitive to other people's feelings, and possesses a sense of humor. From the point of view of economic convenience, Lily Bart and Lawrence Selden cannot "afford" each other. In other words, neither can afford to satisfy their basic human need, which amounts, in the circle of aristocrats they drift in and out of, to marrying for love—a word, by the way, which is conspicuously absent from this novel. Selden is aware, from the opening pages of the narration, of Lily's existential qualities, but more acutely aware of her value as merchandise, as a luxury beyond the reach of his modest salary.

> Everything about her was at once vigorous and exquisite, at once strong and fine. He had a confused sense that she must have cost a great deal to make, that a great many dull and ugly people must, in some mysterious way, have been sacrificed to produced her. (*HM* 9)

Much like Newland Archer in *The Age of Innocence,* Selden is one of Wharton's oscillators, a man who hovers between confusion, as in the above lines, and certainty as evidenced a few pages later when he observes Lily's impeccable grooming.

> He watched her hand, polished as a bit of old ivory, with its slender pink nails, and the sapphire bracelet slipping over her wrist. . . . She was so evidently the victim of the civilization which had produced her, that the links of her bracelet seemed like manacles chaining her to the fate. (*HM* 11–12)

The reader is not allowed to forget, of course, that girls of the past century did not choose, but were chosen—especially girls who did not have mothers to negotiate for them. Lily is forced to wage battle on both sides of the camp, so to speak; though she is compelled by social custom to wait for Selden to make his move, she cannot lose time in her pursuit of a dull, naive aristocrat in need of a wife, the lifeless object of Lily's interest for a good portion of the novel. But Selden is slow in coming to the realization, a few hours too late to do Lily any good, that he loves her and wants to marry her.

> But at least he had loved her—and been willing to stake his future on his faith in her—and if the moment had been fated to pass from them both before they could seize it, he saw now that, for both, it had been saved whole out of the ruin of their lives. (*HM* 351)

With a tragic irony worthy of the Greek classics, Wharton casts Selden as her unwitting spokesman against determinism; like Buriden's Ass, Selden has choices but lacks will, and ends up with nothing but an illusion. The irony is twofold, however, as it is her spokeswoman for free will who dies in the end; Lily has the will to choose but must wait to be chosen. As she waits for Selden to make up his mind her faith wavers or, rather, as Wharton stresses in the novel, Lily's belief in Selden's faith wavers. In the penultimate chapter of the novel the words "belief" and "faith" constitute a *leitmotiv*.

> Yes—but it had taken two to build the nest; the man's faith as well as the woman's courage. Lily remembered Nettie's words. . . . Her husband's faith in her had made her renewal possible—it is so easy for a woman to become what the man she loves believes her to be: Well—Selden had twice been ready to stake his faith on Lily Bart; but the third trial had been too severe for his endurance. (*HM* 341)

William James discovered by experience that doubt and uncertainty produce neuroses and that faith is curative. One of his strongest arguments for belief in free will was based on the healthful benefits of such a belief, but of more importance was his conviction that "in its inner nature, belief, or the sense of reality, is a sort of feeling more allied to the emotions than to anything else."[10] Wharton traces the emotional life of her heroine in depicting her gradual decline in health through loss of faith, loss of belief that her will was her own, and in so doing offers the reader the "causal" element of Lily's death; the twinge of final causation is the absence of curative faith resulting in ill health, lack of sleep, and the need for a drug to give her rest.

The novel is structured, archetypally speaking, as a myth of the fall (from prosperity to proverty), of a dying god (in our case the "hidden god" of inherited wealth), of death and sacrifice, and of the isolation of the heroine. And in adherence to the canons of this archetype, the action takes place in the autumn and winter. Spring, instead of rebirth, brings death: "The next morning rose mild and bright, with a promise of summer in the air. The sunlight slanted joyously down Lily's street" (*HM* 345) . . . but not on Lily.

What I would like to suggest is that by having Lily die "accidentally on purpose," Wharton subtly tells us that from the point of view of narrative that is structured around strong ideas, one can deal with both society and the self without falling victim to pat endings. In other words, the author deftly eludes the closed structure that "the death of the heroine" would normally be expected to produce, by entering the unresolved philosophic controversy of free will vs. determinism—thereby producing one of the most subtle examples of the open-ended novel. The reader is left with very mixed feelings concerning Wharton's heroine: First, with the impression that Lily was fated or predestined to die tragically but was somehow morally responsible for her own death,

> She knew the strength of the opposing impulses—she could feel the countless hands of habit dragging her back into some fresh compromise with fate. . . . If only life could end now—on this tragic yet sweet vision of lost possibilities (*HM* 343);

and second, that society is in some way responsible for the turn of events, as Selden thinks it is.

> He saw that all the conditions of life had conspired to keep them apart; since his very detachment from the external influences which swayed her had increased his spiritual fastidiousness, and made it more difficult for him to live and love uncritically. (*HM* 350-51)

Neither (or both) of these hypotheses are true, and Wharton can be said to embrace James's idea of the "fringe of consciousness" out of which the will makes selections, giving attention to one stimulus rather than another.

> The ideas [consciousness], as mere representatives of possibility, seem set up midway between them [the mind and the given] to form a sort of atmosphere in which Reality floats and plays. The mind can take any one of these ideas and make it its reality—sustain it, adopt it, adhere to it. But the mind's state will be Error, unless the outer force "backs" the same idea. If it backs it, the mind is cognitive of Truth; but whether in error, or in truth, the mind's espousal of the idea is called Belief. The ideas backed by both parties are the Reality; those backed by neither, or by the mind alone, form a residuum, a sort of limbo or no-man's land, of wasted fancies and aborted possibilities. (*RA* 170)

Though his *Pragmatism* was not published until 1907, James had been reasoning pragmatically all along, in *Principles* as well as in *The Varieties of Religious Experience* (1902). James's pragmatism assumes an ever-changing universe. Absolute truth can exist only in a completely created and fixed universe in which every event is predestined from the beginning, a role Wharton ascribes in her novel to the old-moneyed aristocracy governed by absolute truths about themselves. This is not the sort of universe we experience; the one we do experience, James maintained, is "a pluralistic, restless universe, in which no single point of view can ever take in the whole scene; and to a mind possessed of the love of unity at any cost, it will, no doubt, remain forever inacceptable" (*DD* 136). Wharton's novel gives this philosophical statement a time, a place, and a name; in her universe the future is still uncertain, and human effort may tip the scales for good or ill. Hence the danger and uncertainty of the world in which Lily Bart lives; hence also the need for human courage in building a better social order. Ultimately Wharton, like James, is less a metaphysician than a moralist. Both, however, are consummate literary artists.

NOTES

[1]Ludwig Lewishon, *Expression in America* (New York, 1932) xxix.

[2]Grace Kellogg, *The Two Lives of Edith Wharton* (New York: Appleton, 1965) xiv.

[3]Edith Wharton, *The House of Mirth* (1905) (London: Virago Press, 1990). Hereafter cited in the text as *HM*.

[4]M.M. Bakhtin, *Speech Genres and Other Late Essays* (Austin: University of Texas Press, 1986) 23.

[5]Diana Trilling, "*The House of Mirth* Revisited," *Harper's Bazaar* 81 (1947), reprinted in *Edith Wharton: A Collection of Critical Essays,* ed., I. Howe (Englewood Cliffs, N.J.: Prentice-Hall, 1962) 105–106.

[6]Bruce Kuklick, *The Rise of American Philosophy* (New Haven: Yale University Press, 1977) 164. Hereafter cited in the text as *RA*.

[7]George Santayana, *The Genteel Tradition,* ed. D.L. Wilson (Cambridge, Mass: Harvard University Press, 1967) 40.

[8]Edith Wharton, *The Age of Innocence* (1920) (New York: Penguin Books, 1974) 280.

[9]William James, "The Dilemma of Determinism," in *The Will to Believe and Other Essays in Popular Philosophy,* eds. F. Burkhardt and P. Bowers (Cambridge, Mass.: Harvard University Press, 1979) 122. Hereafter cited in the text as DD.

[10]William James, "The Perception of Reality," in *The Essential Writings,* ed. B.W. Wilshire (Albany, N.Y.: State University of New York Press, 1984) 133.

10. THE YELLOW RIVER TURNING BLUE, THE YELLOW RIVER TURNING RED: "HE SHANG" AND THE "CULTURAL CRAZE" MOVEMENT

Balance T. P. Chow

The Yellow River! Its water comes from the sky;
It rushes into the ocean and it will not return.

—Li Bai

Your bodies died, but your spirit is divine!
Your souls will be champions among the dead!

—Qu Yuan

"Their ancestor is the Yellow Emperor. . . . Their water is yellow, their earth is yellow, and their race is yellow. . . . It seems the very color of their skin has been dyed yellow, by the Yellow River. . . . For thousands of years, the Chinese have held onto the yellow soil and turned their backs to the blue sky, earning their livelihood from the land. . . . The yellow soil embodies thousands of years of culture. It has acquired a mystic quality, as if it envelops the very soul of the Chinese"[1]

from "He shang"

BEHIND THE COLOR SYMBOLISM of these statements, quoted from the script of the television series "He shang," there is a considerable amount of iconoclastic rhetoric.[2] All the references to yellowness, perhaps, point to the character of Chinese culture as emblematized by a peasant who has never stepped beyond his village in all his life. As he explained to the filming crew, "My parents haven't given me the guts to do that" (HS 61). It is this kind of "yellow-earthliness" in Chinese civilization that "He shang" seeks to cure through relentless exposé.

This is no doubt a formidable task. Intended to be a project of "social engineering" never attempted before, "He shang" offers diagnoses and prescriptions involving difficult issues of economic, political, historical, and cultural significance preoccupying the minds of officials and peasants, intellectuals and illiterates alike in recent years.[3] In this paper, I will review the contents of the series and situate it in the context of the "Cultural Craze" movement that gave birth to the program.

"He shang" consists of six parts, each lasting about thirty minutes. The review below will concentrate on its narrative.

Part One, written by Su Xiaokang, is subtitled "In Search of a Dream." It points out that Chinese civilization, nurtured by the Yellow River over the millennia, has been suffering from a loss of vitality for the past few hundred years. Despite the decline the Chinese, as their indefatigable cult of the dragon suggests, are still dreaming of a perennial empire. They should have awakened from such a dream even as early as the Kang zi years, when the West began to pose serious challenges to Chinese civilization. Citing historians such as Toynbee, Wittfogel, and K. C. Chang (HS 15, 17) to characterize Chinese civilization in terms of the Asiatic mode of production, the narrative warns that some of the world's major riverine civilizations have been eclipsed or vanquished by the industrial civilization of the West. Apparently there is only one way out: since the Yellow River has become senile and sterile, a new Chinese civilization has only industrialization to take as a point of departure.

Part Two, subtitled "Destiny" and written by Wang Luxiang, attempts to pin down the essential character of Chinese civilization from the perspective of cultural geography. The narrative begins by identifying the "Middle-Kingdom complex" as the psychological obstacle to the construction of modern China as an "open" country.[4] This problem is a result of an earthbound mentality developed by the Chinese over the ages.[5] Geographical barriers around the country and the self-sufficiency of the Yellow River basin have given rise to a mechanism of self-enclosure that typifies the Yellow River's culture. And it serves the Chinese so dutifully that their civilization has survived continuously for thousands of years—ironically at the price of stagnation, conservatism, inflexibility, and resistance to foreign cultures. The Great Wall, a national symbol, is a monument to this mechanism, and rhetorically, the narrative asks the audience, "Why are the Chinese so fond of walls that they even built one along the eastern coast?" While the coastal wall failed as a means to keep out Japanese pirates in the Ming dynasty, it is nevertheless symptomatic of the efforts to exclude the "oceanic civilization" of the Western powers coming of age in the sixteenth century. The agrarian civilization of China might have eventually absorbed the nomadic barbarians but failed to adequately respond to foreign challenges arriving from across the oceans.

Part Three, "Sparks of Genius," written by Wang Luxiang, focuses on the predicament of intellectuals throughout Chinese history. The story of ancient Chinese civilization, as epitomized by many scientific inventions and discoveries that still have considerable impact on the West, is essentially the glory of China's intellectuals. The question, then, is why the "sparks of genius" have been dimmed and extinguished on native soil after the 17th century. Reading the history of the Tang dynasty hermeneutically, the narrative asserts that a sense of confidence and openness during the Tang dynasty allowed China to absorb and digest foreign culture to her own benefit, but that such an attitude has been lacking in modern times because of overdevelopment of the Confucian ethic and underdevelopment of the Confucian ethic and the

127

underdevelopment of the scientific spirit. Commenting on the neglected tombs of ancient scientists and inventors, and the subhuman treatment teachers and intellectuals have received in contemporary China, the narrative directly associates the decline of Chinese civilization with a lack of recognition for the sanctity of scientific knowledge itself.[6]

In Part Four, "The New Era," written by Zhang Gang and Su Xiaokang, the question asked is, "Why hasn't industrial civilization, which implies tremendous wealth, appeared in Chinese history?" The narrative suggests that absolute despotism, with its ideology of "centralized authority" and "grand-scale unity," has prevented the emergence of private ownership and hence capitalism and industrialization.[7] The consequences of a centralized system of political and economic power are illustrated with appalling statistics that testify to China's economic underachievement.[8] The narrative subsequently encourages the Chinese to join the world market, reassuring them that economic reform is on the whole a necessity even though lack of a mechanism for "opportunity, fairness, and competition" has caused temporary hardships.

Part Five, "Distressing Predicament," is written by Su Xiaokang.[9] Taking the Yellow River both as a concrete problem and as a metaphor, this section attempts to correlate the periodic flooding of the Yellow River with social upheavals recurrent in Chinese history, usually at the turn of dynasties. The common denominator between the two kinds of disasters is a cyclical pattern known as "periodical cataclysm." Following a theory developed by Jin Guantao and Liu Qingfeng in their book *Xinsheng yu weiji* (*Prosperity and Crisis*), the narrative attributes the vicious circle of social upheavals to the "ultrastable structure" of Chinese society itself.[10] According to this theory the stagnancy of Chinese civilization is a function of the periodic devastation of Chinese society, in the process of which progressive elements are eliminated by "disorganized forces" that are produced both structurally and institutionally. Progressive elements are wiped out once these forces have brought about destruction and Chinese civilization (like Sisyphus) returns to where it started from, only to begin the entire process anew. Prescribing a means to short-circuit the destructive cycle, the narrative suggests a "sense of crisis" and a "historical wisdom" to be learned from critical "reflection" (*fan si*).

Part Six, "The Azure," written by Xie Xuanjun and Yuan Zhiming, provides a more concrete conception of how the "distressing predicament" described earlier can be overcome. Beginning with an adoration of the azure ocean, the narrative goes on to contrast riverine civilizations with oceanic civilizations represented by ancient Greece, renaissance Europe, Japan, and the modern West in general. While marveling at how "capitalism powered the twin wheels of the industrial revolution and free trade, initiated great advances, and inaugurated the historical dual chorus of science and democracy" (HS 90), the narrative laments the failure of China's repeated efforts in modernization and the downfall of intellectuals advocating such projects. As Zhuang Zi's Taoist parable about the ignorance and complacency of the Yellow River god He Bo suggests, it is only when the Yellow River meets the ocean that China will be cleansed of her muddiness and cured of her shallowness (HS 93). Concluding the program, the narrative highlights the importance of respect for intellectuals and calls for an end to authoritarianism and dictatorship.

Approved by the government at first, "He shang" was a phenomenal success and could very well have been the crowning jewel in contemporary Chinese culture. However, the series was banned shortly after its broadcast and condemned by a second ban after a brief reprieve, and it remains a monstrous eyesore to the authorities. Nevertheless, to millions of viewers "He shang" represents a cultural breakthrough in that it is one of those very few historical moments when intellectual concerns and popular interests meet as one. Seen from a broader perspective, the moment is also a high point in the "Cultural Craze" movement.[11]

The movement began as a purely academic activity in 1982 in Shanghai, where two symposia on the theme of Chinese cultural history were held, the first of that nature to take place since the establishment of the People's Republic of China. The primary purpose of these two conferences was to discuss how a history of Chinese culture should be written. However, by 1984, as economic reform (a policy in effect since 1979) was beginning to affect the day-to-day life of every Chinese family, the focus of such academic activities gradually shifted to concrete realities. Important themes began to emerge, such as the nature of contemporary Chinese society, comparisons between Chinese and Western culture, and the problems of tradition (ZW 21). In 1985 in large cities such as Shanghai, Beijing, Guangzhou, and Wuhan, strategies concerning cultural reform as an integral part of economic reform were also put on the agenda, and "cultural surveys" were conducted on a large scale. Although "culture" is a broad term, at this point the Chinese had something rather specific in mind. At the fundamental level, the Chinese were concerned about such questions as, What kind of aesthetics should be developed for the increasing amount of commodities if such products are to successfully hit the international and domestic markets? Apart from monetary incentives, how could workers be motivated to increase their productivity? To improve the efficiency of management, what knowledge and mentality should managers and officials be encouraged to acquire? Given the increasing populations in cities, what kind of activities should people be encouraged to engage in after work so their energies could be organized to benefit economic reform in the long run? To this end, what kind of facilities should be given priority for development? How many television sets and radio-cassette recorders should be produced? In short, given the dramatic changes brought about by economic reform, the major concern was how the cultural outlook of society at large could be engineered synchronically to accelerate the project and minimize resistance.

In its initial phase, the "Cultural Craze" movement was essentially a program officiated by the government, and as such it was a supplement to the economic program. Ironically, however, a new theme gradually emerged and began to exert pressure on the state ideology—that modernization entails not only technological advances and an improved economy but also cultural change. As the movement unfolded, "Cultural Craze" manifested itself in various phenomena and on different levels. For instance, there was tremendous demand for books, movies, electronics, consumer items, and luxury goods such as cosmetics. Many clubs and leisure groups engaging in activities such as reading, stamp collecting, horticulture, and so on were formed, providing people with opportunities to associate, the political implications of which should not be too difficult to imagine. The pool of intellectuals also expanded dramatically as people began to reaffirm the value of higher education (which has been devastated by the Cultural Revolution) and to eagerly compete for enrollment in the relatively small, though rapidly increasing, number of colleges and universities. More significantly, "Cultural Craze" opened up the possibility of serious reflections on the inherent problems on the Chinese cultural tradition and the way this tradition was hindering the progress of modern China. Chinese culture became an object of critique in academic and intellectual circles. "Wen hua fan si," which literally means "reflective thinking about culture," soon became a catch phrase. Analogous to the Nietzschean concept of the "transvaluation of values," reflective thinking created an arena in which discourses on subjects other than Marxism and socialism became a possibility.

Once "wen hua fan si" was introduced, the "Cultural Craze" movement entered a new phase. This new development created a united front for two kinds of critics. On the one hand, high-caliber dissidents, including loyal members of the communist party, began to appear and to make themselves heard. The three most significant figures, Liu Binyan, Wang Ruowang, and Fang Lizhi, who have now been stripped of their party memberships, began to challenge the official ideology— not because they really wanted to overthrow the political orthodoxy at the time, but because the Communist government had become corrupt and needed purification.[12] Opinion that the Marxist concept of alienation also applies to socialist countries perhaps epitomizes the challenge from within the political orthodoxy.[13] On the other hand, from academic circles and the think-tank of economic reform also emerged a number of intellectuals who began to explore new paths of inquiry.

Several examples can be given here. The first is Li Zehou, one of the consultants of the video program. Li, a renowned scholar generally known for his studies in aesthetics, was at the time becoming increasingly influential as a result of his recent work in Chinese intellectual history.[14] In an important essay on the May Fourth Movement, Li pointed out that immediate or impending crises such as the Treaty of Versailles and the Sino-Japanese War have always overshadowed the burgeoning need for intellectual enlightenment. For the Chinese, "enlightenment" ("qi meng") would mean long-term re-education of the entire nation to develop a modern mentality, the hallmarks of which are science and democracy. To accomplish this, a transformation of traditional values is necessary. Because the Chinese have been deprived of the Enlightenment, modernization invariably fails because tradition always holds society back.[15] The implications of this theory are that economic reform and technological advances sought by the Chinese government could very well eclipse the call for enlightenment again, and traditional forces could even put a stop to attempts at material modernization itself.

Two more examples are Jin Guantao and Liu Qingfeng, whose training in the social sciences allowed them to address the same problem noticed by Li Zehou, but from a broader perspective and in a more global context. In their many significant works they applied systems theory and cybernetics to the study of Chinese history, which they scrutinized in comparison with the history of the West, by focusing on critical moments such as the fall of the Roman Empire, medieval feudalism, and the rise of capitalism.[16] Their study is encapsulated in the hypothesis of the "ultrastable structure of Chinese society" discussed above in connection with "A Distressing Predicament."[17]

On the whole, whether intentionally or unintentionally, these transvaluative developments in Chinese academia provided a theoretical basis for the program of modernization and economic reform. This theoretical support was very much needed because the economic program was running into difficulties. Inflation, regional differences, conflicts between the socialist and the capitalist sectors, unemployment, corruption, social unrest, and student rallies, to name a few of the problems, indicated that the official ideology was unable to provide proper guidance for the project. While the masses were dissatisfied with the side effects of reform, they were also unwilling to revert to the old system of centralized economy. In short, China had come to a crossroads. It was at this juncture that the "Cultural Craze" movement came closest to achieving enlightenment with political implications. Unlike the masses, who simply grumbled at the soaring prices of daily necessities and the like, intellectuals (most of whom were in fact liberal officials) seemed to believe seriously that the rationality of their discourse carried great potential for overcoming the impasse at the radical—or ideological—level. The strategy some intellectuals adopted, it seems, was to put this possibility to the test by popularizing through a mass medium the visions of the cultural transvaluation movement. Thus, "Cultural Craze" in a sense culminated in what has been called "The 'He shang' Phenomenon." As Su Xiaokang put it, the series was to be a call for the entire nation to do some reflective thinking about their culture.

The call was heard, and the program enjoyed unprecedented popularity when it was aired. However, since the series touched upon various academic disciplines, it also generated considerable debate among scholars in China, Taiwan, Hong Kong, the United States, and other countries.[18] One of the most astute criticisms is perhaps the view that "He shang" is advocating a certain kind of "cultural determinism" which effectively evades the central issue altogether, being that it is not the cultural tradition of China, but rather the political reality of Marxism-Leninism that is in crisis.[19] Although there is some truth in this view, the criticism is possibly misplaced because everyone already knew that politics was the ultimate issue. However, the authors of "He shang" also knew that ideological taboo made it tantamount to suicide

133

for one to grapple openly with the problem on a political level. Whether positively or negatively perceived, the series had started a wide spectrum of people thinking about China's problems past and present—especially problems of immediate interest.

Though still too early to tell, it is possible that the "Cultural Craze" will have far-reaching implications comparable to those of the May 4th Movement of 1919. In the world context of the breakdown of the "master narrative," as Lyotard describes it, the "Cultural Craze" is also analogous to intellectual movements known in the West as "postmodernism" and "poststructuralism."[20] At any rate, immediate significance of the "Cultural Craze" can be glimpsed in the demonstrations that occurred in Beijing, Shanghai, and other cities in the spring of 1989. One would imagine that the general interest aroused by "He shang," which as we have seen was a major event in the "Cultural Craze" movement, could very well have partly fueled the massive involvement of the people, for in retrospect the political call voiced poetically at the end of "He shang" has also been one of the most important messages from those demonstrations.

In the last few moments of "He shang," while the Yellow River is seen flowing into the ocean, merging its yellow with the Pacific's blue, we hear the narrator saying:

> Authoritarian government is characterized by secrecy, dictatorship, and arbitrariness. Democratic government is characterized by transparency, democraticity, and scientificity. We are in the process of going from turbidity to transparency. . . . After a solitude lasting thousands of years, the Yellow River finally sees the open, azure ocean. (HS 98-100)

Clearly, the authors wanted the Yellow River to merge with the ocean, to purge itself of its muddiness and turbidity, and to turn into a transparent blue. It is uncanny that the series of video essays was originally called "The Great Artery," but was renamed "He shang," which literally means "Yellow River's Elegy for Premature Fatalities."[21]

Instead of turning blue, the Yellow River has turned red with the blood of the many who died young in 1989 because of a curse upon their civilization. The martyrs, the authors of "He shang," and the many intellectuals and other individuals for whom they stand, are the tragic heroes who wear this crown of irony for the distressing predicament of Chinese history.

NOTES

[1]Su Xiaokang, Wang Luxiang, et al, "He shang" (Beijing: Xiandai chubanshe, 1988); reprint (Taipei: Jinfeng chubanshe and Fengyun shidai chubanshe, 1988) 10, 24. Hereafter cited in text as HS. The reprint edition, which contains a collection of articles and reviews, is the source for all citations in this paper. The manuscript of an anonymous English translation (which is still imperfect), a copy of which is in my possession from an indirect and unacknowledged source, is probably available at the Fairbank Center for East Asian Research Library of Harvard University. I have adopted, modified, or consulted this translation in passages cited in the paper. The video (two cassettes) is available (without English subtitles) in some video stores operated by Asians in American cities.

[2]"He shang" was first broadcast in 1988, the Year of the Dragon, beginning June 12 in Beijing on the Central Television network of the People's Republic of China. Concerning the actual circumstances of its fortunes and misfortunes, the reader is referred to the following sources: "He shang," especially 169–70; "Long de beicang—guanyu he shang de zhaji," in *Long de beicang—he shang huixiang* (Taipei: Fengyun shidai chubanshe, 1989) especially 63–64, 150 (hereafter cited in the text as LB); Liu Yanying, "Dianshi zhenglunju he shang zhenjing zhongnanhai," *Jingbao yuekan* (1988): 40–42; Frederic Wakeman, Jr., "All the Rage in China," *The New York Review of Books*, 3 (March 2,

1989): 19–21; Nicholas D. Kristof, "China Now Condemns Acclaimed TV Series," *The New York Times* (Oct. 2, 1989): 15, 20.

[3]See Su Xiaokang's preface to "He shang" (HS 6). Su actually described the enterprise as "cultural-philosophical systems engineering," the target of which is to "rebuild the cultural-psychological structure of the Chinese people's national character."

[4]On this complex see Yin Haiguang, *Zhongguo wenhua de zhanwang*, chapter 1.

[5]The earth-bound mentality of the Chinese has been dramatized in two outstanding movies, *Old Well Village* and *The Yellow Earth*, available in many video stores operated by Asians in American cities.

[6]On this problem, see especially the reportage "Shensheng yousi lu" by Su Xiaokang, reprinted as Appendix 2 in "He shang."

[7]It is interesting to note that this interrogation of the absolute, unity, and authority is comparable to deconstruction as it is known in the West.

[8]"The GNP of China ranks among the last 20 countries or so of the 128 countries of the world, i.e., in the company of Somalia and Tanzania. . . . In 1960, China's GNP and Japan's were roughly equivalent, but in 1985 it was only one-fifth of Japan's. The GNP of the United States exceeded China's by $460 billion in 1960, but the difference increased to $3,680 billion in 1985" (HS 63).

[9]The original title, "You huan," is very difficult to translate. "You" basically means "to worry," "worries," and "things to worry about," but the term is loaded with cultural values in the sense that China's intellectuals have a very long tradition of "worrying" (often helplessly) about the well-being of the state on behalf of the people. It is the Chinese equivalent of the sense of the tragic. "Huan" reinforces the meaning of "you," but it can also refer to "pains," "disasters," and "catastrophes." The content of Part Five suggests that what the authors had in mind was both the objective calamities as such and also the imperative sense of responsibility the intellectuals are bound to in the face of disastrous circumstances.

[10]Jin and Liu, *Xingsheng yu weiji* (Changsha: Hunan renmin chubanshe, 1984). Their theory of "ultrastable structure" is also elaborated in *Jin guantao liu qingfeng ji* (Harbin: Heilongjiang jiaoyu, 1988) 69–202. Hereafter cited in the text as JG.

[11]"Cultural Craze" may be a translation with negative connotations not actually contained in the original "wenhua re," which simply refers to people's "heated" enthusiasm about cultural matters. On the "Cultural Craze" movement, see Wu Xiuyi, *Zhongguo wenhua re* (Shanghai: Shanghai renmin chubanshe, 1988). My description of the craze that follows is based on this book.

[12]Concerning their views and opinions, see Liu Binyan, *Liu binyan zi xuan ji* (Hong Kong: Cosmos Books, 1988); Wang Ruowang, *Tian di you zhengqi* (Hong Kong: Baixing, 1989); Fang Lizhi, *Fang lizhi— zhongguo de sha ka luo fu*, eds. Shi Zhongyu and Wang Lili (Taipei, Taiwan: Guiguan, 1987).

[13]This heretical application of alienation was, interestingly, first proposed by Zhou Yang, sometimes known as the "Czar of Contemporary Chinese Literature," in 1964. After being reinstated as the Minister of Culture, he gave a report in 1983 at the Academic Conference on Occasion of the Centennial of the Death of Karl Marx, where he reintroduced the idea claiming that, "we must recognize the existence of alienation before we can overcome this problem." See Jiang Mu, *Sanshi niandai zuojia lun* (Taipei: Dongda tushu gongsi, 1986) 78.

[14]Li Zehou, *Zhongguo gudai sixiang shi lun* (Beijing, China: Renmin chubanshe, 1986); *Zhongguo jindai sixiang shi lun* (Beijing: Renmin chubanshe, 1979; reprint 1986); *Zhongguo xiandai sixiang shi lun* (Beijing: Dongfang chubanshe, 1987).

[15]See Li Zehou, "Qi meng yu jiu wang de xuang chong bianzhou," in *Zhongguo xiandai sixiang shi lun*, 7–49. On the reflective thinking and the May 4th Movement, see the recent anthology of essays by Lin Yusheng, et al., *Wu si: duo yuan de fan si* (Hong Kong: Joint Publishing Company, 1989).

[16]Jin and Liu explained their methodology, JG 13–62.

[17]Jin and Liu adapted the term "ultrastable system" from W. R. Ashby's *Design for a Brain* (JG 80).

[18]See Liu Shuxian, "Sixiang wenhua weiji haishi xianshi weiji?" in *Jiushi niandai*, April 1988, 82–91.

[19]See François Lyotard, *The Postmodern Condition: A Report on Knowledge* (Minneapolis: Univ. of Minnesota Press, 1984) 37–38 *et passim*.

[20]The title "He shang" is generally translated as "River Elegy." Actually, "He" refers to the Yellow River, while "shang," a term used by the poet Qu Yuan (c. 343–290 or c. 335–296 B.C.E.), refers to premature deaths, for example, of young warriors who sacrificed their lives for their country (See LB 4,16).

11. ISHMAEL REED'S POSTMODERN REVOLT

Erik D. Curren

FOR ISHMAEL REED the history of Western culture is one of violence and domination. In his 1972 novel *Mumbo Jumbo,* Reed's unlikely spokesman for "high" art, police chief-turned-art-museum-curator Biff Musclewhite, explains with brutal candor the greatest threat to Western culture:

> Son, these niggers writing. Profaning our sacred words. Taking them from us and beating them on the anvil of BoogieWoogie, putting their black hands on them so that they shine like burnished amulets. Taking our words, son, these filthy niggers and using them like they were their god-given pussy. Why . . . why one of them dared to interpret, critically mind you, the great Herman Melville's *Moby-Dick!!*[1]

Such a passage situates Reed's novel firmly amid the cultural politics of the Western world, politics that Reed engages through the formal devices of his postmodern text.

It has been said that while modernism maintains a strict distinction between literature and society, postmodernism denies any difference between aesthetic and other cultural production. What was really new about contemporary literature for critics of this phenomenon was its rejection of the idea of "high art" held by modernists like Marcel Proust, Thomas Mann, and James Joyce. Leslie Fiedler, for example, proposed in his seminal 1969 essay "Cross the Border—Close the Gap" that postmodernism had developed an anti-art aesthetic, a revised idea of the institution of art allowing for the use of elements of media and consumer culture, which permitted postmodernist works to represent the electronic fragmentation of contemporary life.[2] Accordingly, contemporary art breaks out of the narrow confines of the prison house of bourgeois art and into society, closing the gap between high and popular art, and crossing the border separating the aesthetic from the practical world.

As we know, the attempt to break out of the irrelevance of *l'art pour l'art* is nothing new, and dates back at least to the birth of aestheticism itself in the second half of the nineteenth century. In his *Theory of the Avant Garde* (1974) Peter Bürger identifies this anti-art movement with the European avant-garde of the early part of this century.[3] In contrast to the Anglo-American tradition of aesthetic criticism that equates modernism and the avant-garde, Bürger distinguishes modernism on the one hand as an attack on traditional writing techniques from the avant-garde, and on the other hand as an attack on the concept of art itself. Modernism accepts the autonomy of art from social life and thus plays a contradictory role. While it attempts to criticize society from the outside by projecting the image of a better order (if only negatively, as in the cases of Franz Kafka and Samuel Beckett), it also serves to "relieve the existing society of the pressure of those forces that make for change," the kind of escapism denounced by critics of *l'art pour l'art* (*TA* 50).

The historical avant-garde wanted to escape contradictions of the traditional isolation of art by making art practical in some way. Art "works" such as Marcel Duchamp's ready-mades—his famous print of the Mona Lisa with mustache and beard graffiti, "L.H.O.O.Q.,"—or

Dadaist manifestations, performances of artists in conversations, fist fights, and so forth, aimed at challenging the autonomy of bourgeois art in a true post-modernism practiced well before the end of the modernist period.

More than fifty years after Duchamp and Dada, American literature from the 1960s on has witnessed the appearance of a native avant-garde, in Bürger's sense, an artistic self-critique. What better place to look for a manifestation of the literary attempt to make art social than in minority literatures of the United States? It cannot be denied that works written by Americans of color are intimately involved with the political struggles for freedom and equality waged by many cultural groups. Since the Black Aesthetic movement, explicitly political and historical literature concerned with ethnic and racial oppression and the attempt to establish countercultural traditions has made a noticeable impact on the American literary and cultural scene. Writers like Toni Morrison, Maxine Hong Kingston, and Ishmael Reed have enjoyed considerable popularity due to a kind of postmodern literary pluralism.

If we focus on Reed we find the model of a politically committed writer. A novelist, poet and essayist, editor and publisher, Reed is above all a cultural critic who attempts to realize his vision of cultural pluralism both in his writings and in literary activism. This activism includes several projects to expand the canon of American literature and make it more useful to pluralist social praxis, ranging from the opening in 1976 of the Before Columbus Foundation—a producer and distributor of the works of little-known ethnic writers—to teaching at UC Berkeley, to lecturing around the country and contributing to publications in the U.S. and Europe. Not surprisingly, his fiction is committed to dealing with the historical situation of African-Americans and exploring the possibilities of their culture. From his first novel, *The Free-Lance Pallbearers* (1967)—the story of Bukka Doopeyduk, a would-be black revolutionary lynched after his abortive attempt to overthrow the totalitarian regime of Polish-American strongman Harry

Sam—up to his most recent work, Reed's writing has tried to demystify the politics of race in the United States and beyond.

Mumbo Jumbo, Reed's best known novel, was written on the heel of the cultural upheaval of the late 1960s and deals with many of the cultural issues that had gained wide currency at the time. An avant-gardist work that goes beyond deconstructing realist conventions of coherence and readability to question the existence of art itself as an entity separate from society, *Mumbo Jumbo* tells a variety of stories in a disconnected narrative that resists all attempts to unify it. Alternately overlapping and parallel stories center on the encounter of two kinds of cultural organization in the history of the West: hierarchical order based on rationality, and egalitarianism founded on folk tradition. Reed focuses on a particular moment of this conflict, the United States of the 1920s, to construct his "main" plot, an allegory of the rise and fall of African-American culture associated with the Harlem Renaissance.

This flowering of black culture is represented by a psychic epidemic called "Jes Grew," named for the haphazard and undirected development of the black folk tradition from scattered cultural roots. The infection represents a threat to the straight-laced American cultural establishment because it causes people to eschew hard work for dancing, singing, and the celebration of bodily existence. Beginning in New Orleans, the cradle of American jazz culture, the epidemic spreads across the country toward New York, seeking what is cryptically referred to throughout the novel as "its text." On the way Jes Grew infects people of all racial, ethnic, and class groups, making them healthy by negating the control exercised over them by rationalism. About Jes Grew, the narrator tells us that "actually, it was an anti-plague. Some plagues caused the body to waste away; Jes Grew enlivened the host" (*MJ* 6).

Despite its salutary effects, or rather because of them, the white rationalist mainstream—led by the Atonist Path, a conspiracy controlling all aspects of society and culture—sees Jes Grew as a disease that threatens all social order. Reed notes that, "To some if you owned your own mind you were indeed sick but when you possessed an Atonist mind you were healthy" (*MJ* 24). To put down the epidemic, the Atonist hierarchy mobilizes its "military arm," the "Wallflower Order" (standing for the Ivy League, as Gates notes), to direct the 1915 United States invasion of Haiti, aimed at the immediate source of Jes Grew, and to sanitize American culture.[4] In an example of the kind of bold anachronism that powers much of Reed's humorous critique, the Wallflower Order in turn calls on the Knights Templar, known for their success in an earlier campaign of Western cultural imperialism, the medieval crusades. The scheming Grand Master of the Templars, Hinckle Von Vampton sets himself up as a patron of black arts in order to wage a disinformation campaign intended to dissipate the power of Jes Grew by turning its most likely carriers into black lumpenproletarians. Toward the end of manufacturing a false black consciousness friendly to the domination of white Western culture, Von Vampton publishes a literary rag sheet aimed at the black audience. This journal, aptly named *The Benign Monster*, features pornography and romantic depictions of street violence along with commentary demonstrating that black culture, when it gets beyond the usual primitive forms, is entirely derivative of the European High Art tradition.

Meanwhile Papa LaBas adept at African-inspired HooDoo, uses his arsenal of conjures to aid the spread of the "anti-plague" in hopes that it will liberate the whole country from the domination of rationalism and its repressive morality. From his Mumbo Jumbo Kathedral, LaBas, a man whom we are told carries Jes Grew inside him like other people carry DNA, uses a combination of HooDoo loas and Western science to challenge the power of Atonist alienated consciousness by getting people in touch with the pre-scientific side of their bodies and minds.

The plot of Jes Grew is crossed by threads of connected subplots, which, taken together, create an account of Western cultural history from early Egypt through the 1920s and up to the civil rights movement of the sixties in a narrative that self-consciously mixes fiction and fact. Reed's book attempts simultaneously both to demystify the history of

143

the West and to explore the possibilities of African-derived culture in postmodern society. In Reed's history, art plays a key role in the struggle between scientific and traditional systems of morality. Early in the history of the West scientific thinking shattered the unity of traditional society, represented for Reed by an idyllic vision of ancient Egypt.

> In Egypt at the time of Osiris every man was an artist and every artist a priest; it wasn't until later that art became attached to the state to do with it what it pleased. (*MJ* 164)

What the state did with art was either to turn it into propaganda or to seal it off from political life through the ideology of High Art, both moves serving to bolster a social order that justifies state rule.

Far more interesting to Reed than an explicitly propagandistic use of art is the cultural imperialism involved in the attempt to generalize Western autonomous art as universal High Art. Since the Atonists define the dominant culture and control its dissemination through print and electronic media, it is the European classics that are held up as "the most notable achievements of mankind" (*MJ* 57). Art museums— Centers of Art Detention—serve to enforce a useless kind of aesthetic autonomy, separating both the Western classics and "primitive" art from social praxis. The novel explores two contradictory methods of liberating art from detention, philosophies of avant-garde praxis that represent the two paths open to African-American literature, both in the twenties, the time of the Jes Grew story, and in the seventies at the time of Reed's own writing.

The first method of artistic liberation involves the physical removal of Third World artworks from Western museums by a multicultural gang of artnappers, who represent a strategy of using violence against the established order. They use people as tools in their projects, as when they kidnap Musclewhite, the director of the Center of Art Detention, in order to get a Toltec head for ransom, and by so doing they practice the instrumental and violent morality developed by Atonism itself. Thus discredited, violent separatist cultural activism takes a back seat to an explicitly non-instrumental practice whose spokesman within the novel is Papa LaBas, and whose model is the synchronic practice of Reed's own novelistic strategy in *Mumbo Jumbo*.

The novel's self-assertion as social praxis relies on the avant-garde negations of art that constitute Reed's text. Aside from deconstructing the conventions of literary realism, a move that postmodernism inherits from modernism, *Mumbo Jumbo* departs from even the modernist novel through its use of discursive forms from outside the genre. The addition of illustrations, footnotes, and a bibliography to its fictional text situates *Mumbo Jumbo* between novelistic, academic, and print media discourse. The "Partial Bibliography" at the end of the book stands out as a key avant-gardist device with several functions. Aside from challenging genre expectations and complicating the distinction between fiction and fact, the bibliography plays another, contradictory role. The placement of a bibliography at the end of a fictional text certainly parodies both scholarly claims to authority, as Gates notes (BB 706) and the literary use of cultural documentation by the white modernism of T.S. Eliot and Ezra Pound. But, at the same time, the bibliography attempts to do real historical and anthropological recovery work, harnessing the prestige of academic knowledge to support its critique of rationalism and its promotion of the African-American narrative tradition.

Reed insists on the need for African-American culture to maintain all its traditional sensuality and to resist the pressures of Western instrumental reason and pragmatism in general, but within the post-industrial West in which it has been placed, and not in a quixotic return to premodern idyllic unity. In the modified speech-act terminology of Jean-Francois Lyotard's theory of society in *The Postmodern Condition* (1979), black culture for Reed is a separate "language game" from white culture, a body of knowledge with different rules and different criteria for determining value.[5] For Reed, black culture is what Lyotard defines as traditional or narrative culture, a fluid social arrangement that thrives on many kinds of knowledge, all of which seek an egalitarian encounter with nature and with people in society. In the industrial age narrative is opposed to science, the positivistic quest for mastery that characterizes dominant white culture for Reed.

The encounter of modern science with narrative is for Lyotard an unequal one, which explains the failure of Jes Grew to generalize itself at the end of Reed's tale. This inequality is due to the relative openness of narrative over science; while traditional narrative culture tolerates all sorts of knowledge, even science itself, scientific enlightenment on the other hand denounces narratives as archaic mystifications, "fables, myths [and] legends, fit only for women and children" (*PC* 27). Like Reed, Lyotard sees this "unequal relationship . . . [as] the entire history of cultural imperialism from the dawn of Western civilization" (*PC* 27). The history of cultural domination recounted in *Mumbo Jumbo* is the antagonism between positivism, geared toward efficiency, and narrative culture where people and things are not means but ends in themselves.

However, this antagonism obtains only for positivism, the scientific discourse of the industrial modern period whose goal is efficiency. In postmodernity, Lyotard claims the dominant mode of science is not logical but "paralogical," relying not on a universal system of rationality based on consistency and identity, but on local explanations that take account of paradoxes and indeterminacy. This postmodern thinking is realized today in disciplines like quantum physics and catastrophe theory and microphysics that undertake not only to question and revise previous scientific knowledge, but to challenge the very category of science itself and its separation from narrative.

This is a very avant-garde move, and it parallels the challenge to Western rationalistic culture made by Reed. Yet, here we see that what was in one sense an avant-garde revolt on Reed's part was also an assertion of a certain kind of aesthetic autonomy from social praxis. In the Atonist-dominated world of *Mumbo Jumbo* the whole spectrum of social praxis, from repatriating Third World art to invading Haiti, is governed by bourgeois rationalism and the modern drive toward efficiency. Thus, all pragmatic measures use people as instruments, making them into various means towards various ends. To resist dominant reason, Reed insists on the autonomy of his text from achievable political programs. Like Lyotard, Reed sees modern science and narrative as two separate language games, with different rules for validity. Only when society abandons the drive toward mastery and efficiency, and makes a space for paradox, can Reed envision the congruity of science and narrative, and consequently, of black and white. Until then, if "then" ever comes, art must stand in a critical relation to society, and African-American culture must lead the way to a democratic and pluralist postmodernism.

While Reed's program of making no compromises with (white) dominative reason comes from a specifically African-American direction, being an attempt mainly to take the political and aesthetic separatism of figures like Amiri Baraka into a more productive direction, it risks sharing the same fate as the European avant-garde of the twenties, namely, falling into the very elitism and obscurantism that it wanted to transcend. While many a reader who has been nursed on self-conscious classics of the modernist canon will delight in Reed's erudite allusions, irrelevant anachronisms, and narrative twists, what sort of reader is excluded from the pleasure of the text? Perhaps it is just the sort of person who is subjected to the intimating claims of a culture that snubs her, a culture whose high art is constructed to keep her in her place, a place more often than not in front of the TV. Of course, it is simple to tag a highly original writer as elitist, and the aesthetic imperatives of a reductive socialist realism that underlie this move are a fundamentally unproductive frame through which to interpret any avant-garde work.

Just because the audience for *Mumbo Jumbo* will always be more or less limited does not necessarily consign the book to a politically quietistic aestheticism. However, the very powerful critique that Reed's text launches against practical reason, like Lyotard's prescription for postmodernity, is so utopian that standard political action of any sort is reduced to a common denominator of zero. Not merely is all activist praxis dominative, but history appears to be an unending repetition of the fight between binaries that never never transcends the fundamental structure of antagonism. Thus, Osiris vs. Aton, Jes Grew vs. Puritanism, Eros vs. Thanatos, and noble savages vs. the men who would be king are all conflicts explained by the cyclical view of history expounded at the end of the book: "Time is a pendulum. Not a river. More akin to what goes around comes around" (*MJ* 218).

NOTES

[1]Ishmael Reed, *Mumbo Jumbo* (Garden City, NY: Doubleday, 1972) 114. Hereafter cited in the text as *MJ*.

[2]Leslie Fiedler, "Cross the Border—Close the Gap." Report in *The Collected Essays of Leslie Fiedler* Vol. 2 (New York: Stein and Day, 1971) 461-85.

[3]Peter Bürger, *Theory of the Avant-Garde* Trans. Michael Shaw, foreword Jochen Schulte-Sasse (Minneapolis: U of Minnesota Press, 1984). Hereafter cited in the text as *TA*.

[4]Henry Louis Gates, Jr., "'The Blackness of Blackness': A Critique of the Sign and the Signifying Monkey" *Critical Inquiry* 9 (1983): 685-723. Hereafter cited in the text as BB.

[5]Jean-Francois Lyotard, *The Postmodern Condition: A Report on Knowledge,* trans. Geoff Bennington and Brian Massumi, foreword by Frederic Jameson (Minneapolis: U of Minnesota Press, 1984). Hereafter cited in the text as *PC*.

12. ADAPTATION, HISTORY, AND TEXTUAL SUPPRESSION: LITERARY SOURCES OF HITCHCOCK'S *SABOTAGE*

Thomas Hemmeter

IN REACTING AGAINST AHISTORICAL textual readings of films, the field of cinema studies embraces the historical analysis of films both as products of historical forces and as producers of historical perspectives. Such studies generally examine the production practices of studios, the social conditions of audiences, and the economic and ideological pressures on filmmakers and the film industry. While this historical criticism does valuable service by filling in the historical context, sometimes the textual history of the film is neglected. Filmed adaptations of literary sources are particularly fertile sites of textual history since the films express both historical evaluations of their own periods and historical re-evaluations of the earlier period producing the literary source. A third historical period is implicated as well—that of the film criticism analyzing filmed adaptations. Dudley Andrew reminds us that in their own making of history, critical analyses are not above history—there is a historical dimension to their discourse.[1] In examining all three historical dimensions of Alfred Hitchcock's *Sabotage*, adapted from a Joseph Conrad word, it is clear that the critical discourse has worked to repress certain aspects of the film's textual history.

In 1907 Joseph Conrad published a novel entitled *The Secret Agent*. In 1936 Alfred Hitchcock directed and released a film entitled *Sabotage*. (He could not title his film *The Secret Agent* because he had used that title for his film adaptation of Somerset Maugham's *Ashenden* released the same year.) From 1965 to 1990 the critical conclusion has been that the Conrad novel is the single literary source of the Hitchcock film. Why Hitchcock chose to adapt such a dense, gloomy novel dominated by a sardonic narrator when he had success with more popular literary sources published between 1915 and 1935 remains a minor puzzle to most Hitchcock scholars. Tom Ryall notes that the novel preceded the popular cycle of spy thrillers which began around 1914 with World War I and continued into the 1930s.[2] Why would Hitchcock seek out a difficult text by an unpopular, if highly respected, writer concerned with pre-war social and political malaise?

One obvious answer to this question is found when noting historical parallels between the Edwardian decade building to World War I and the 1930s decade building up to World War II. Another possible answer to this question is that Hitchcock may not have gone back only to the 1907 novel; he may have also used as a source the play *The Secret Agent*, which Conrad adapted from his own novel. This intervening text complicates the easy equation of Edwardian and 1930s England. The absence of this dramatic adaptation of Conrad's novel in the discussion of Hitchcock's adaptation choices in *Sabotage* is a significant gap in the critical discourse (including Hitchcock's own) on the novel. I will argue that this discourse gap is also a historical gap, and that a textual history of the adaptation process evident in *Sabotage* reveals filmmaker and critics to be engaged in a type of history making which Pierre Sorlin, analyzing historical films, calls an effort to define their own vision of the past.[3] In the case of *Sabotage* a crucial aspect of this critical history making is the suppression of the intervening dramatic text of *The Secret Agent* in the discussion of the film's literary sources. A study of filmed adaptations reminds us that history is an act of forgetting as well as remembering.

Conrad adapted the play *The Secret Agent* from his novel in the years 1919–22, and it enjoyed a short run on the London stage in November, 1922.[4] The historical facts regarding Conrad's play strongly suggest that Hitchcock saw the work on stage. Hitchcock is known to have been a habitué of the London theater and to have been in London when Conrad's play was staged.[5] The only critic to cite Conrad's drama *The Secret Agent* as the literary source of *Sabotage*, Donald Spoto also notes Hitchcock's habit of inveterate theater-going.[6] One suspects the common critical preference for the Conrad novel as the literary source to have something to do with a preference for a more respectable precursor text: the novel enjoyed at least limited critical success (TL 878), while the play had a mercifully short run and was not critically admired.

An examination of the text of the play reveals details which give it claim, along with the novel, as one precursor text of *Sabotage*. The overall contours of the novel's plot remain in Conrad's play: the domestic tranquility of Verloc, an inactive double agent, his wife Winnie, and her retarded brother Stevie is disturbed by the demand from Verloc's superior that he sabotage the Greenwich Observatory with a bomb; the bomb's premature explosion prompts the police, Verloc's anarchist colleagues, and the reader to investigate what happened, leading first to the false conclusion that Verloc blew himself up and then to the realization that Stevie lost his life when Verloc sent him with the bomb; and when Winni Verloc discovers finally that her brother has died, she kills Verloc and finally herself after she is betrayed by another anarchist. (The play has her go mad rather than commit suicide.) The chief difference between novel and play is the latter's focus on the Verlocs, eliminating the saturnine narrator and much of the material on anarchists and double agents. The generic requirements of drama require a more condensed narrative, leading Conrad to announce that, in adapting his novel for the stage, he decided to focus on Winnie instead of Verloc, the secret agent (TL 838).

The film reproduces this focus on Winnie as the central member of a love triangle, like the play producing a discourse which places personal relations in the foreground at the expense of the novel's broad political and social issues. The film removes what little remained in the play about political matters, moves the Verlocs from a pornography shop to a movie theater, and blends the police investigator and the anarchist lover of Winnie into one character. The film's major alteration is in plot: Where both novel and play have the bomb explode about one-third of the way through and lead us through investigations in which we are partially in the dark, the film delays the bombing until two-thirds of the way through and focuses on the aftermath—Winnie's reactions and those of her policeman-lover. The film also does not have Winnie commit suicide or go mad; instead, it has her joining a gay crowd of Londoners with her unwelcome lover.

Though the two precursor texts seem to offer the same basic narrative to adapt, there are some telling details in Conrad's play which mark it as a source. The stage directions specifically describe Stevie as dressed in an apron to do domestic chores,[7] a detail that does not appear in the novel but does appear in the film. The explosion in the movie theater at the end of *Sabotage* is another variation from the novel which the play anticipates in a line from an anarchist who dismisses just such a plan as ineffectual, "Blow up churches, theaters full of people— that's no good"(DT 35). And we can easily imagine a line from the play like "the police can do nothing" (DT 57), ringing in Hitchcock's head. Many other references or verbal images which echo in Hitchcock's film—the repeated use of the carving knife Winnie uses to kill Verloc or the reference to Stevie's death as accidental, "as if he had been run over by a bus" (in the film he dies in a bus)—appear in both novel and play, but stand out more forcefully in the latter since they are not embedded in the novel's dense text.

The argument here is not for a greater fidelity of film to play than to novel. Indeed, Conrad's novel includes details which might be argued to be inspiring certain film events. For example, during a famous scene in *Sabotage* Verloc, instructed to bomb Picadilly Circus, visualizes the destruction when the fish tank he has been staring at in an aquarium dissolves into an image of collapsing structures. The novel's narrative describes a character's imagination of a bomb's destructive power as "the overlighted place changed into a dreadful black hole belching horrible fumes choked with ghastly rubbish of smashed brickwork and mutilated corpses".[8] No lines from the play convey the imaginative fears of characters so visually.

Though one may find many parallels between film and novel, the ignored play stands as another source precisely because it expresses a historical pattern of textual suppression. In adapting his novel for the stage, Conrad suppressed most of his novel's overt political material; in adapting novel/play for the screen, Hitchcock suppressed most of the overt references to sex and buried the political material even more deeply than the play had done. Anarchists, foreign agents, and revolutionaries become shadowy figures, clearly elements of a MacGuffin, the plot pretext which creates external conflicts about which the characters are concerned but the viewer is not. This process of narrative suppression (MacGuffinizing), begun by Conrad's play which greatly reduces the role played by political agents in the novel, is continued in the film.

The film also expresses material that both Conrad's novel and play suppressed: the actual killing of the boy. The novel has the bombing simply happen in a narrative ellipsis, which has the effect of hiding the killing itself. In the play, Act 2 and part of Act 3 are concerned with people all talking about the bombing, but the real concern is not the event but the consequences for Winnie and for others in British society. Hitchcock's film reverses the emphasis: suppressing the broad social effects, *Sabotage* shows the gradual movement towards the boy's death itself. The effects of his death are narrow, focused on Winnie and her lover. Like all adaptations, which both preserve and cancel out the original text, *Sabotage* both conceals and reveals material from its predecessor text. The suppression of the dramatic text—by Conrad, by

Hitchcock, and by critics discussing *Sabotage*—extends this textual process.

The critical history of the film text reveals a similar pattern of expression and suppression. The credits cite Conrad's novel as the literary source, and the two book-length works on Hitchcock's British films both assume that Hitchcock adapted his film from Conrad's novel (AH 126-127).[9] Even articles focused specifically on the nature of Hitchcock's adaptation in *Sabotage* assume that Conrad's novel provided the director with his source material.[10] Never mentioned (except in the critical biography by Spoto) is the fact that there are two Conrad works entitled *The Secret Agent*. The 1922 play, a source closer in time, is also more closely related in spareness of structure and in medium to the 1936 film than is the novel. Yet the critical heritage assumes that Hitchcock, who by 1936 had adapted ten plays into films and who suffered some studio pressure to use popular plays as source material (AH 179, passim), adapted *Sabotage* from the single novelistic source.

Without the intervening dramatic text to complicate historical assumptions, critics of *Sabotage* are free to dehistoricize the film into a typical studio adaptation with no firm relation to any historical period. On the one hand, its relationship to Edwardian England is denied; Hitchcock's film is "more reflective of [his] own time and place than of Conrad's".[11] On the other hand, its relationship to the social realities of England in the 1930s is denied; it is one of a vogue of spy thrillers and melodramas which hint "unwittingly" of events abroad.[12] Part of this critical project to dehistoricize *Sabotage* has to do with that common habit in adaptation criticism, privileging the literary source text and marginalizing the derived film text, which Eric Rentschler notes has the effect of overlooking vast intertextual space between film and source.[13]

A facet of this critical practice is the assumption of a unitary, coherent predecessor text, in this case Conrad's novel. A corollary assumption is that there is a direct historical link between the novel's fictional events and those of the Edwardian period. With a single preceding text as an anchor, the twenty-nine years between the novel and the film become unified—an uncluttered linear skin stretched over the intertextual space between film and novel. This historical simplification allows easy ideological parallels; e.g., as Conrad's novel is concerned with international and social problems leading to World War I, Hitchcock's film is concerned with problems leading to World War II. The 1930s assumes a profile similar to that of the Edwardian period, and the historical conclusion is that Britain repeated its mistakes or answered its challenges in two traumatic international stuggles. When Conrad's 1922 play enters the picture, however, the easy parallel disappears and the entire forty years from 1900 to 1939 become a complex historical fabric, not two parallel threads in England's political struggle against international chaos and violence.

To shift the discussion from broad historical and political grounds to means of production, it might be argued that the intervening dramatic text has been ignored because of conditions in the British film industry of the 1930s. Tom Ryall's study, *Alfred Hitchcock and the British Cinema*, goes a long way toward anwering what Eric Rentschler argues is a central question of any adaptation study: Why does the artist adapt certain material at certain times (GF 4)? Although Ryall's study examines economic, studio, and artistic influences on Hitchcock's work (AH 85-184), with *Sabotage* he focuses on genre and adaptation. Ryall concludes that Hitchcock, working to produce entertainment films, was bound to a great degree by the conventions of popular art, particularly the thriller genre, whose vogue in the 1930s led the director to choose a number of similar literary properties for adaptation. He places *Sabotage* in what he calls Hitchcock's "thriller sestet": The *Man Who Knew Too Much* (1934), *The 39 Steps* (1935), *The Secret Agent* (1936), *Young and Innocent* (1937), and *The Lady Vanishes* (1938). What binds these six films together is a uniformity of literary source: unlike earlier films derived from middlebrow literary and dramatic adaptations, these six films drew on such traditions of popular culture as the crime and spy novel (AH 179).

But there is an interesting gap in Ryall's account, a gap which suggests that historical studies of films should not be limited to accounts of studio production constraints and of ideological apparatus imposed by economic and sociological conditions of a historical period. Although he draws a clear distinction between *Sabotage* and *The 39 Steps*—the latter has a dark tone derived from Conrad's novel while the former is light in tone because it adapts a popular novel—a unifying impulse leads Ryall to erase his own distinction and lump Conrad's novel in with other popular novels. Ryall's privileging of popular sources as one reason for Hitchcock's superior 1930s films requires the marginalization of middlebrow literary sources, as he mentions in particular dramatic adaptations (AH 128, 131-32). It makes sense, then, that as he suppresses the historical and textual differences of Conrad's novel from the other five suspense novels which Hitchcock adapted—the novel *The Secret Agent* was earlier in time and hardly popular—Ryall also suppresses the dramatic text of *The Secret Agent*. The play constitutes a middlebrow dramatic adaptation, though unsuccessful, and Ryall describes such adaptations as studio-enforced mechanisms to which Hitchcock had to flee when personal projects failed in the 1925-1933 years (AH 173). The 1922 text of *The Secret Agent* had to be suppressed.

> *Truffaut:* Making a child die in a picture is a rather ticklish matter; it comes close to an abuse of cinematic power. *Hitchcock:* I agree with that; it was a grave error on my part.[14]

In discussing with Francois Truffaut his decisions to have a young boy blown up by a bomb in his 1936 film *Sabotage*, Hitchcock typically backs away from a violation of audience expectations, apologizing for alienating his viewers' sympathies. This is a common Hichcock maneuver, as we find him, for example, apologizing for his film experiments in *Rope* (HI 130-31). Of course, Hitchcock loved technical experiment and indulged this interest in many films besides *Rope*, just as he indulged the habit of killing off attractive characters in films besides *Sabotage* (e.g., *Psycho*, *Vertigo*, *Frenzy*). Indeed, Hitchcock often complains about studio decisions demanding that a killing be suppressed or that a handsome leading man be declared innocent, as in the changed endings of *The Lodger* and *Suspicion*. Despite his disclaimer, in killing the innocent boy in *Sabotage*, Hitchcock succeeded in expressing what he wanted. His later confession of regret may be seen as an attempt at suppression.

Naturally Hitchcock does not correct Truffaut's assumption that *Sabotage* is based on Conrad's novel (HI 75), as indeed it was in part. The critical suppression of the less respectable literary source, a failed play, itself an adaptation, is met by Hitchcock's own suppression. One motive has to do with the ambivalence (or downright hostility) of British studio executives in the 1920s and 1930s toward art films, which may have lent some respectability to a film but were at odds with commercial success (AH 89). One distributor in particular, C. M. Woolf, came into conflict with Hitchcock more than once because he "nurtured a suspicion of Hitchcock's artistic qualities" (AH 164). Hitchcock would be safer claiming a novel distant in time—its unpopularity forgotten, its author famous enough to lend some prestige to the film—than to claim a pretentious play which was known to have not drawn an audience.

Another motive for Hitchocock's suppression is his own ambivalence toward drama. Though he thought that dramatists are more skilled than novelists in adapting their material for the screen (HI 50), in a sense the closeness of film to drama presented him problems in adapting plays. Hitchcock needed to narrate dramatic materials in cinematic form and felt embarrassed over his version of *Juno and the Paycock* because it resisted cinematic transformation (HI 48; LT 104-105). Indeed, Hitchcock claimed he felt he had stolen something when he was praised for *Juno*, leading him to declare his intention to avoid literary masterpieces; his preferred method was to read a story once, forget the material and start to create cinema (HI 48-49). Suppression of the original text—he was unable to remember the story material drawn from sources on which his films are based—was clearly a working method for Hitchcock. It is an easy extension of this working method to see Hitchcock repressing a play like *The Secret Agent* whose discourse, closer to that of film, would resist his imaginative translation.

As in his statement on killing the child in *Sabotage*, Hitchcock's words are not entirely to be trusted. Suppression is so contrived a part of his working methods and his publicity that he also may have suppressed certain debts to Conrad's play. Though known to have worked extensively on scripts for most of his films, Hitchcock never has claimed screenwriting credit. The suppression of the play *The Secret Agent*, beyond the obvious publicity and business value of putting forward the more prestigious novel as the putative source text, expresses Hitchcock's mode of adaptation. To adapt is to conceal certain sources by overtly revealing an obvious source.

The act of Hitchcock and the critics to privilege the novel as the single source text of *Sabotage* is a historical act of suppressing other predecessor texts. In discussing the discourse of adaptation in the context of the theory of intertextuality, Christopher Orr challenges the notion of a singular literary source as a determining pretext for a filmed adaptation. A literary source is one of a series of pre-texts showing the same narrative conventions as the film adaptation. "The act of adapting a text from another medium is, in effect, the privileging or underlining of certain quotations within the film's intertextual space".[15] Orr would have us look at cultural codes and ideological practices in the adapted film's production as well as comparative discursive practices to guard against reductive discussions of fidelity of film to literary source. What is fascinating in the case of *Sabotage* is that studies like Ryall's of *Sabotage*'s conditions of production lead to conclusions similar to those of critics applying the discourse of fidelity of film to novel. Neither approach uncovers the historical document of the intervening third text, the play *The Secret Agent*, which challenges the singular notion of a literary source more definitively.

In *The Film in History*, Pierre Sorlin notes that "history is a society's memory of its past" and that each society creates its own version of the past according to its social organization (FH 16-17). Important in this historical memory, of course, is forgetting; in the process of selecting certain events, encounters, and documents to remember, others are selected to be forgotten. In discussing the literary source of *Sabotage*, film critics of the 1960s, 1970s, and 1980s have decided not to recall the intervening dramatic text of *The Secret Agent* and instead to remember the Conrad novel, joining Hitchcock in creating an oversimplified version of *Sabotage*'s textual history. Dudley Andrew says that history is not a sequence of events but "the revaluation by which events are singled out and understood in successive eras" (CF 127). The suppression of Conrad's play as a source of *Sabotage* extends Andrew's notion. As an adapted text, *Sabotage* has been revalued by successive generations who have chosen to foreground one facet of its textual past, its debt to the Conrad novel, and efface another facet, its debt to the failed Conrad play. The full complexity of the film's intertextuality has not been singled out for historical memory. Adaptations present history as an act of forgetting as well as remembering.

NOTES

[1]Dudley Andrew, *Concepts in Film Theory*, Oxford: Oxford University Press, 1984. Hereafter cited in the text as CF.

[2]Tom Ryall, *Alfred Hitchcock & the British Cinema*, Urbana: University of Illinois Press, 1986. Hereafter cited in the text as AH.

[3]Pierre Sorlin, *The Film in History: Restaging the Past*, Totowa, New Jersey: Barnes & Noble, 1980. Hereafter cited in the text as FH.

[4]Frederick R. Karl, *Joseph Conrad: The Three Lives*, New York: Farrar, Straus and Giroux, 1979. Hereafter cited in the text as TL;

Jocelyn Baines, *Joseph Conrad: A Critical Biography*, New York: McGraw-Hill, 1960.

[5]John Russell Taylor, Hitch: *The Life and Times of Alfred Hitchcock*, New York: Pantheon, 1978. Hereafter cited in the text as LT.

[6]Donald Spoto, *The Dark Side of Genius: The Life of Alfred Hitchcock*, Boston: Little, Brown, 1983.

[7]Joseph Conrad, *The Secret Agent: A Drama in Three Acts*, London: T. Werner Laurie, 1923. Hereafter cited in the text as DT.

[8]Joseph Conrad, *The Secret Agent*, 1953 Anchor edition. New York: Doubleday, 1907.

[9]Maurice Yacowar, *Hitchcock's British Films*, Hamden, Connecticut: Archon Books, 1977.

[10]Michael Andregg, "Conrad and Hitchcock: *The Secret Agent* Inspires *Sabotage*," *Literature/Film Quarterly* III, no. 3 (Summer 1975): 215-225; Goodwin, James. "Conrad and Hitchcock: Secret Sharers." In *The English Novel and the Movies*, edited by Michael Klein & Gillian Parker, 218-227. New York: Ungar, 1981.

[11]Steve Vineberg, "Two Routes into Conrad: On Filming *Under Western Eyes* and *Outcasts of the Islands*," *Literature/Film Quarterly* XV, no. 1 (January 1987): 22-27.

[12]Tony Aldgate, "Ideological Consensus in British Feature Films, 1935-1947." In *Feature Films as History*, edited by K.R.M. Short 94-112. Knoxville: University of Tennessee, 1981.

The view that Hitchcock's 1930s films do not reflect socio-political reality is widely held, supported by film historian like Roy Armes. Critics like Furhammar and Isaksson (139), attempting to counter that view, nevertheless feel constrained to put films like *Sabotage* in the suspense genre, a category whose structural demands weaken the film's political impact. Sam Simone, who devotes a book to establishing Hitchcock's overt political intentions in the 1940s films, agrees that his 1930s films were not as ideologically open because of governmental and studio censorship as well as the suspense structures (22). Hitchcock tried to warn the United States against Nazi sabotage in the 1940s films, but *Sabotage* is not a prior effort to rouse the English to the Nazi threat because it is seen as a part of a generic pattern of thriller adaptations and thus politically irrelevant. See: Roy Armes, *A Critical History of British Cinema*, London: Tantivy Press, 1977; Leif Fruhammar, and Folke Isaksson. *Politics and Film*, Translated by Kersti French. New York: Praeger, 1971; Sam P. Simone, *Hitchcock as Activist: Politics and the War Films*, Ann Arbor: UMI Research Press, 1985.

[13]Eric Rentschler, "Introduction: Theoretical and Historical Considerations," In *German Film and Literature*, ed., Eric Rentschler (New York: Methuen, 1986) 1–8. Hereafter cited in the text as GF.

[14]Francois Truffaut, *Hitchcock*, New York: Simon & Schuster, 1967. Hereafter cited in the text as HI.

[15]Christopher Orr, "The Discourse on Adaptation," *Wide Angle* VI, no. 2 (1984), 72-76.

13. WHAT MOVIE ARE WE WATCHING HERE? CINEMATIC QUOTATION IN RECENT HOLLYWOOD FILMS

Linda Anderson

POSTMODERNIST WRITERS HAVE constructed literary texts with multiple beginnings and endings, interspersions of nonwritten material, and even attempts to present "several texts more or less simultaneously."[1] "More or less," however, seems to be as close as literature can come; true simultaneity seems to be denied to the writer and the reader, reserved instead for the producers and viewers of performed texts. One example of multiple texts presented simultaneously occurs in recent Hollywood movies that "quote" older films by cannibalizing and recontextualizing fragments of these films.[2] The "quoted" films are most often Hollywood classics of the 1930s, 1940s, and 1950s, which the viewers and the characters of the embedding film watch simultaneously; the quotations are frequently concerned with topics introduced or emphasized in modernist texts, including sexuality, psychology, science and technology, and criminality (LH 35). But while the films in which the quotations are embedded may seem to resemble postmodernist literary texts in their appropriation and use of fragments of earlier works, the differences in media and audience response may cause cinematic quotations to be read very differently from literary ones.

Although different filmmakers use quotations in different ways, all films that use such quotations are, inevitably, set in a time after the films they quote. The use of quotations grounds the more recent films in a time frame in which movies are available; a costume drama such as *Dangerous Liaisons* (1988) obviously cannot use such quotations if it is to maintain the illusion of being a realistic depiction of eighteenth-century events. The particular movies quoted are, by definition, part of the culture available both to the characters of the later films and those films' audiences. What, if anything, such quotations mean in their new contexts is largely dependent on viewers' knowledge of the older films, their reactions to such films, and their ability or willingness to apply their knowledge and reactions in new contexts.

The use of fragments of older films in more recent ones privileges the reader/viewer by allowing greater latitude of interpretation than is usually possible in a written text. A written quotation usually represents a pause in the narrative. The reader must first attempt to read the quotation; if the quotation is in a language unknown to the reader, a gap in understanding the writer's intention must result unless the writer has provided a translation, in which case a further pause results while that engages the reader. Next, the reader must interpret the meaning of the quotation. Then the reader may want to search his or her memory for the source of the quotation, unless the writer has provided that information. Finally, the reader may want to interpret the quotation in its new context. The effect of a filmed quotation may be very different, since the main action usually does not stop while the quotation is running. The viewer may therefore choose where to direct his or her attention: to the main action, to the quotation, or to both—simultaneously or serially. Or the viewer may not even be cognizant of the quoted fragment; the source of the quotation may or may not be mentioned; characters in the main action may allude to the quotation or what it means, or they may not. In any event, something is going on to which the viewer may or may not be paying attention, either joining the characters of the main action in the real-time experience of viewing the film or experiencing the film as background to the main action. There need not be a pause, and the viewer need not feel excluded if he or she does not recognize the source of the quotation or the reason(s) the filmmakers have incorporated it into the more recent film.

Self-referentiality in films is, of course, nothing new. Warner Brothers cartoons of the 1930s and 1940s parodied popular actors and actresses: Katharine Hepburn as Bo Peep, Charles Laughton and Clark Gable (in their *Mutiny on the Bounty* roles) as two of the *Three Men in a Boat*. New Wave filmmakers often draw upon cinematic tradition—particularly of Hollywood films of the 1930s and 1940s—in the films they make, and films in genres such as western and horror often refer to conventions established by earlier films in their genres.[3] In contrast to these films, however, popular Hollywood films seem to use fragments of older films largely as decoration. A knowledge of and ability to recognize the source, original meaning, and recontextualized meaning of these fragments is usually necessary if the quotation is to enrich the audience's experience of the more recent film. Therefore, unless such quotations are merely inside jokes, background noise, or irrelevant counternarrative, a certain cinematic literacy is assumed on the part of at least a portion of the audience. On the other hand, since these quotations are generally not necessary to the narrative of the more recent film, less knowledgeable or alert viewers will presumably not feel cheated if they do not "get" the quotation. A knowledge of the American *film noir* tradition is necessary to understand Jean-Luc Godard's intentions in *Breathless* (*À bout de souffle*, 1960); a familiarity with *A Guy Named Joe* (1943) is not necessary to understand Tobe Hooper's intentions in *Poltergeist* (1982).

Frederic Jameson has suggested one kind of decoration for which recent Hollywood filmmakers have mined older films and recycled the fragments:

> Modernism was predicated on the achievement of some unique personal style which could be parlayed out to the subject of genius, the charismatic subject, the superscript if you like. If that subject has disappeared, the styles linked to it are no longer possible. A certain form of depersonalization thus seems implicit in all of this: . . . even when modernism is pastiched, it is only an imitation of style, not style.[4]

The 1988 horror film *The Kiss* explicitly acknowledges the glamour of an earlier film when Amy Halloran (Meredith Salenger) visits her mother's friend Brenda (Mimi Kuzyk), who is watching *Blond Venus* (1932) on TV. The scene quoted is a nightclub act featuring a Hollywood version of an African tribal setting; a gorilla appears, but reveals itself to be a disguised Marlene Dietrich, who strips off the gorilla suit and sings, "Hot voodoo, I'm aflame/I'm really not to blame. . . ." When the adolescent Amy asks, "How come she's dressed up like a gorilla?" the older Brenda replies, "style." This quotation may be read as a way of developing Brenda's character—a woman who enjoys watching stylish old movies—as a means of establishing a relationship between Brenda and Amy, whose mother has recently died, or as a method of establishing our identification with these characters (if we also enjoy such movies). The quotation may also be read, however, as a fragment mirroring aspects of the movie in which it is embedded. Amy's Aunt Felice (Joanna Pacula), stylish in a 1980s fashion, has already been revealed as having become a vampire during her childhood in Africa, and, as she later tells Amy, she collects African talismans. Although she may not be to blame for her transformation she, like the disguised Dietrich, is not what she appears to be and ultimately strips away her disguise. A further parallel is that Dietrich's character, as Brenda tells Amy, "sleeps with [Cary Grant]"; Felice will ultimately conduct an affair with Amy's father. Although the use of this quotation is ingenious, its function is purely ornamental, and the viewer who does not make these connections can still understand and enjoy the embedding film.

Films in the postmodern era often are pastiches, as their use of film quotations from a variety of genres makes obvious. *Gremlins* (1984), for example, contains quotations from *It's a Wonderful Life* (1946)—both are Christmas films; from *Invasion of the Body Snatchers* (1956)—both are horror films; from *To Please a Lady* (1950)—both are action films featuring a central character who drives a racing car; and from *Snow White and the Seven Dwarfs* (1937)—both are fantasies featuring small animated characters. *Earth Girls Are Easy* (1988), a pastiche of science-fiction, comedy, and romance, quotes from *Beauty and the Beast* (1946), *Earth vs. the Flying Saucers* (1956), *Gun Fury* (1953), *Jungle Manhunt* (1951), *The Nutty Professor* (1963), and *Rebel Without a Cause* (1955). *Crimes and Misdemeanors* (1989), a drama that includes comic, romantic, and crime-story elements, quotes from *Francis the Talking Mule* (1950), *Happy Go Lucky* (1942), *The Last Gangster* (1937), *Mr. and Mrs. Smith* (1941), *Singin' in the Rain* (1952, soundtrack only), and *This Gun for Hire* (1942). Some of the films quoted are relatively obscure, and it is unlikely that any but the most cinematically literate viewers would recognize more than the age and genre of the film (an old romantic comedy, an old gangster film). Others of the quoted films are likely to be more familiar; and even if viewers do not recognize the film or the significance of the particular quotation (if any), they may recognize James Dean or Edward G. Robinson and make their own associations. In all of these recent films, the quotations may be read as serving more than one purpose: they may help set the tone, establish character, foreshadow coming action, or serve as segues between narrative strands, but their purpose remains primarily decorative; they are playful additions to the narrative, not essential elements of it.

Single elements of popular Hollywood films may also be extracted from their original contexts and used to trigger audience associations, as in the excerpts in *Crimes and Misdemeanors* from the soundtrack of

Singin' in the Rain. Barry Levinson quotes only dialogue from *Sweet Smell of Success* (1957) in *Diner* (1982), in which a minor character wanders through the movie reciting lines from the earlier film; in *Rain Man* (1988), the same director quotes a different element from the same earlier film, when the picture portion of *Sweet Smell of Success* is visible on a TV screen, although the dialogue is indistinguishable. One of the most commonly quoted elements is music: *Tin Men* (1987) quotes the theme from *The Man Who Shot Liberty Valance* (1962) during a revenge scene; *Troop Beverly Hills* (1989) quotes the theme from *The Way We Were* (1973) during scenes when characters are considering their romantic relationships; and *K–9* quotes the theme from *Jaws* (1975) when the dog who plays one of the leading roles in the film is trying to sneak into his human co-star's bed. Another area often quoted is film advertising. In *Good Morning, Vietnam!* (1987), a large poster of James Dean is visible behind the rebellious hero, Adrian Cronauer, during one of his confrontations with an army officer. The heroine of *An American Werewolf in London* (1981) has a *Gone with the Wind* (1939) poster in her living room. Marquees advertising *The Birds* (1963) and *Cattle Queen of Montana* (1954) decorate *Tin Men* and *Back to the Future* (1985), respectively.

Viewers may not notice or recognize any of these quoted elements, and even if they do, their reactions may vary; they may accept the quotations as hints the filmmakers are dropping as to how the audience should read what is happening in the more recent film, or they may reject attempts by the filmmaker to link recent and earlier films. Two 1989 films demonstrate how quotations may be read either as homage or as a way of establishing critical distance (MP 96). In *My Stepmother Is an Alien*, in order to demonstrate the concept of "kiss" to the alien who calls herself Celeste Martin (Kim Basinger), her companion, Bag, shows her old movie clips of, among others, Humphrey Bogart and Ingrid Bergman in *Casablanca* (1942), Gary Cooper and Jean Arthur in *Mr. Deeds Goes to Town* (1936), Marilyn Monroe blowing a kiss, Rudolph Valentino and Agnes Ayres in *The Sheik* (1921),[5] and Cary

Grant and Grace Kelly in *To Catch a Thief* (1955). Viewers may simply enjoy Celeste's attempts to imitate the various kinds of kissing she sees, or, recognizing some or all of the quotations, they may read these fragments as alluding to a Hollywood tradition of romance, which they may either accept as establishing a context for the more recent movie's love scenes or reject as artificial and old-fashioned, or they may accept some as truly romantic and reject others as laughable. A more complex example occurs in *Great Balls of Fire!* After Jerry Lee Lewis (Dennis Quaid) storms out of the house on their wedding night, Myra (Winona Ryder) is shown watching TV and crying over the parting of Horatio Nelson (Lawrence Olivier) and Lady Emma Hamilton (Vivien Leigh) in *That Hamilton Woman* (1941), followed by the logo for the "Million Dollar Movie" and the theme music from *Gone with the Wind* (1939). At this point Jerry Lee enters, picks Myra up, and sweeps her off to their bedroom. The scene from *That Hamilton Woman* is obviously intended to reflect Myra's romantic yearnings and her fear that her husband will not return, but the quotation of the music and its relation to the main action are more interesting. Viewers who do not recognize the quotation can still understand what is happening; but viewers who do identify the *Gone with the Wind* theme may also recognize that Jerry Lee's behavior at his entrance echoes a famous scene from that movie. Such recognition allows viewers to read Jerry Lee and Myra as modern-day parallels to Rhett Butler (Clark Gable) and Scarlett O'Hara (Leigh) or to reject the proposed parallels as absurd.

The use of quotations, particularly of multiple quotations, in recent Hollywood films would seem to echo the discontinuity characteristic of many postmodernist literary texts (LH 43–44; RP 45). The use of a quotation from an older film is in no way determined by the genre or narrative in which the quoted material originally appeared; quotations from dramas may reappear in comic contexts, and vice versa. The films quoted may be famous or obscure, or the quotation may consist of an isolated element of the total film commodity. Quotations serve a variety of associative uses, even—occasionally—structural uses, and single quotations may have multiple uses, or even represent, in Ihab Hassan's phrase, "a double view," potentially both honoring and criticizing the works from which they are extracted.[6] Yet the eclecticism and taste for pastiche shared by postmodernist literary texts and recent Hollywood films may be misleading; because film is capable of simultaneity, discontinuity centers not in the text, but—potentially—in the viewer, who may be unable or unwilling to attend to or recognize everything that is simultaneously going on. And, unlike literary work, a film text does not wait to be read and reread; the viewer must decide where and on what to focus attention. Films, therefore, put more time pressure on the viewer than a reader may feel, while at the same time offering more interpretive choices. However, because cinematic quotations in recent American popular films are seldom if ever integral to the narrative, the pressure is eased, and the play of free choice is expanded.

Postmodernist writers often refer to both history and literary texts as palimpsests (LH 46; QP 32), and this concept might seem to apply as well to films. Use of quotations in recent popular American films, however, seems to bear greater resemblance to the playful decorations of initial letters in illuminated medieval manuscripts, alluding sometimes to the text and sometimes to associated traditions, but often seemingly done for the sheer enjoyment of both the illuminator and the reader.

NOTES

[1]Douwe W. Fokkema, *Literary History, Modernism, and Post-modernism,* The Harvard University Erasmus Lectures, Spring 1983, Utrecht Publications in General and Comparative Literature, 19 (Amsterdam and Philadelphia: John Benjamins, 1984). Hereafter cited as LH. For an interesting discussion of the possibility of simultaneity in narrative, see Susan Stewart, *Nonsense: Aspects of Intertextuality in*

Folklore and Literature (Baltimore: Johns Hopkins University Press, 1979) 146–70.

²I would like to thank Roberta Green for alerting me to several of the quotations mentioned in this paper.

³Roy Armes, *French Cinema* (New York: Oxford University Press, 1985). Hereafter cited as *FC*. For New Wave referentiality, see *FC* 17–76 and Silvio Gaggi, *Modern/Postmodern: A Study in Twentieth-Century Arts and Ideas* (Philadelphia: University of Pennsylvania Press, 1989) 89–97.

⁴Stephanson, Anders, "Regarding Postmodernism: A Conversation with Frederic Jameson" in *Postmodernism/Jameson/Critique*, ed. Douglas Kellner *PostModernPositions* 4 (Washington, D.C.: Maisonneuve Press, 1989) 43–74. Hereafter cited as RP.

⁵Since the film credited is the compilation *The World's Greatest Lover* (1977), and only a few seconds of Valentino as sheik are shown, it may be that the film quoted is *Son of the Sheik* (1926) and the actress with Valentino may be Vilma Banky.

⁶Ihab, Hassan, "The Question of Postmodernism." *The Performing Arts Journal 16*, 6 (1981): 30–37. Hereafter cited as QP.

14. THE CINEMATIC ADAPTATION: THE CASE OF *LOS SANTOS INOCENTES*

Patricia Santoro

THE CINEMATIC ADAPTATION of a literary text provides yet another valuable tool in the teaching of literature. For both student and teacher, analysis of the relationship of the written work to its cinematic version offers a fresh point of departure for textual study. Both verbal and visual narratives are actualizations of similar communication systems, for each is motivated by the desire to tell stories and create images. The verbal text organizes linguistic tools (phonemes, graphemes, tropes, syntax, and semantic shadings) to create images and meaning. The adaptation of the verbal text uses cinematic tools to transpose meaning and image to the screen. Pictorial composition, sound, *mise-en-scène*, choice of actors, and technical equipment are among the elements that structure the visual rendering of an original text. The analysis and comparison of both works serve to enrich their study in the following manner: (1) each text is valued as a distinct cultural artifact that relies on its own set of tools to create meaning; (2) rich artistic and aesthetic possibilities are revealed by the reconciliation of both novel and film; and (3) an understanding is reached of what these two art forms share.

Los santos inocentes was written by the Spanish author Miguel Delibes in 1981. It was adapted for the large screen in 1984 by Spanish director Mario Camus. Both texts portray the lives of landless peasants living in virtual serfdom in Extremadura, Spain, in the 1960s. The prolongation of a medieval-style class structure until as late as the third quarter of the twentieth century was in part a result of weak agricultural policies enacted during the dictatorship of Francisco Franco (1939–1975). This anachronistic socio-political situation is brought to life in the story of a single peasant family, common laborers on the estate of a family of absentee landlords. An oppositional social plane is represented by the presence of the landlords, who visit the estate for occasional hunting forays and religious ceremonies.

Analysis of two segments of the film and their respective relationships to the original text demonstrates the various ways in which meaning can be transposed from the literary text to the cinematic text. The first segment, one of two pre-narrative moments, deals with one member of the peasant family, Azarías, a mildly retarded man in his sixties. Azarías is a legendary figure among the peasants. His unpleasant habits include never washing, urinating on his hands, and defecating capriciously, although not maliciously, on the grounds. He is barefoot and toothless and his clothes are filthy. He speaks little, repeats set phrases, is very much in his own world, yet is intelligent enough to value the small tasks he performs on the estate. Azarías is a gentle giant, a Saint Francis figure who tames and communicates with wild birds. The first pet presented in both texts is a wild owl, whom he treats like a loving wife. The second bird is a little jackdaw, who lights on his shoulder on command. The plot structures of both film and novel create parallel stories of peasants and landowners. In both cases, it is Azarías and the landowner Iván who bring the stories to their climaxes. Iván, a voracious and relentless hunter, kills the little jackdaw in an outburst of sheer frustration after a fruitless day of hunting. In retaliation, the inconsolable Azarías hangs Iván by tricking him under a tree and slipping a noose around his neck.

174

The segment showing Azarías (the first of the two prenarrative sequences) occurs before the presentation of the opening credits and introduces the viewer to several crucial thematic elements of the narrative. The Azarías sequence attempts to approximate a passage in the novel that describes the fear that both Azarías and his pet owl feel toward the tawny owl (*el cárabo*), whose cry Azarías associates somehow with the abyss. Azarías makes periodic forays into the hills to chase the tawnies both for the sake of his pet owl and to quell his own fears. When his pet is sick, and the landowners laugh at Azarías's request to call in a local faith healer, the reader learns that the retarded man associates the landowner's laughter with the cry of the tawnies and therefore with the deep, dark, and fearful unknown. This association affords the reader a crucial insight into the psychological underpinnings of the retarded man, while also providing a stronger motivation for the murder of Iván.

The prenarrative segment consists of a series of shots juxtaposed in rapid montage. A framed close-up shot of an owl (this is Azarías's pet owl) opens the sequence. A voice is heard on the sound track shouting "ieh! ieh!" Then a medium shot of Azarías appears. He has been calling the tawny and is motionless, waiting for a reply from his nemesis. When he hears the owl hoot in reply, Azarías's face is consumed with joy. This image of Azarías is that of a large, powerful man and reflects a characteristic suggested in the original text. The strong torso (in the novel Delibes called it "hercúleo" [herculean]) seen in this image looms against the pale sky, and the childlike, guileless expression inscribed on the obviously older face provides an instance of iconography reminiscent of another cinematic adaptation, that of Mary Shelly's novel, *Frankenstein or the Modern Prometheus* (1818), in James Whale's 1939 film *Frankenstein*. Azarías is indeed the gentle but dangerously misunderstood "monster." The surreal aspect of this sequence approximates not only a narrative moment from the novel, when "the moon came out from behind the skyscape and flooded the countryside with a surreal phosphorescence populated with shadows," (SI 20–

21, all translations mine) but also the *tone* of this moment, a difficult achievement for any adaptation.

Azarías calls again and begins to run. The camera cuts back to the pet owl, who responds by moving nervously on the tree branch. Delighting in his powers of communication, Azarías is again seen running, and again a shot of the owl appears on the screen. The camera then cuts to Azarías running quickly through the brush. The image track begins to speed up, expanding story time in order to emphasize the surreal aspect of this moment. The image of Azarías becomes blurred and confused. The entire segment creates a disturbing element that contradicts the gleefulness we first witnessed in the old man, and it underscores the disparity between his actions and his age. The strategic presentation of this disquieting element before the opening credits of the film represents an attempt to approximate the prose of the original and thus support a crucial theme, that of the fear Azarías feels toward the tawny owl. When he heard the owl, "Azarías lost the notion of time and of self, and, crazed, he began to run" (SI 21). Here, the film uses a cinema-specific code (the speeded up image track) to attain yet another unnatural effect (the first was Azarías as Frankenstein figure) and works to undermine the gentleness and passivity of the retarded man. At the same time the adaptation approximates the statement made in the novel that Azarías feared the laughter of the tawnies, laughter associated with the laughter of the masters, which signified for him the abyss. It is this abysmal difference (the deep and the dark as well as the insurmountable) between the landowners and the peasants that is central to the meaning and narrative development of the novel. Enunciation of this theme at the beginning of the film text emphasizes the ideological adhesion of the adaptation to the original. As the sequence draws to a close, two levels of non-diegetic music are heard on the soundtrack: a loud, menacing drumbeat and the nervous jangling of a tambourine. Their effect is to reinforce the frenetic quality of the scene for the viewer and to concretely support the narrative moment by simulating the heartbeat and nervous system of the running man. The film cautions the viewer, before the story has taken shape, to be aware of the negative and dangerous elements to follow.

At the end of this sequence the screen fades to white, and the second pre-narrative sequence begins. This second sequence is quite brief, consisting of the exposure of a photograph of a peasant family—the film's protagonists. The fade to white (the cinematic code is usually fade to black) is a structuring device used four more times throughout the film. Its use is an attempt to imitate the structure of the original text. The verbal text in *Los santos inocentes* is 176 pages long and is divided into six segments labeled as "books." The announcement of each book ("Libro Primero," for example) is delivered on a single page and is followed by its identifying title ("Azarías," for example). In this way the reader experiences both a new beginning and a sense of closure at six intervals during the narrative. The fade to white in the film introduces four narrative segments, four flashbacks ostensibly authorized by four of the characters. The novel's sense of repeated openings and closure is thus imitated by the openings and closings of the four flashback segments. The narrations contained in the flashback sequences take place approximately one year after the murder of Iván, the climactic event that brought closure to the novel. The structural change that organizes the adaptation serves to create a new and crucial temporal level, one that adds a more positive ideological value to the new text. The positioning of the film's narrators a year or so after the events of the novel implies that, as a consequence of the landowner's death, the son and daughter of the peasant family have left the medieval conditions of the estate to forge a new life in the larger towns.

Each flashback is preceded by an exposition of the character's present circumstances. The moment immediately preceding the transition from present to past consists of an establishing long shot focusing on the character; this image then overlaps and dissolves into a medium close-up; another overlap shot dissolves into a close-up; the camera then rests on the pensive face of the narrator. This camera technique literally functions to bring the viewer closer to the narrator in order to

177

share his or her thought processes. As the camera pauses for an instant on the narrator's face, his or her thoughts occur aurally on the soundtrack, and the sound bleeds over from one cut (the present) to the next (the past) in the editing process. This motif, repeated in all four flashback sequences and in several other transitional scenes, known as a dangling diegetic signifier, functions to unify the film's organizational structure and to create a cohesive story flow for the viewer.

For example, when we are introduced to the first flashback sequence, that of the son of the peasant family, Quirce, we see his face and hear "La B con la E hace Be" (the B with the E makes BE). The film cuts from the boy, who in his present circumstances is wearing a soldier's uniform and leaning against a wall in a poor neighborhood of a town, then brings us to a modest room, lit by a single candle, where a pronunciation lesson is taking place. Quirce, who has just been watching several poor children at play in the street, is recalling a time when his father, Paco, was teaching him and his sister Nieves to read. The film, consistent in its intention to add a more positive ideological level to the lives of this family, has chosen to change the original text. In the novel it is Paco, along with his peers, who learns the pronunciation rules. The father struggles yet never quite grasps the many mysteries of the language. The film text transposes the learning process onto Quirce and Nieves, who internalize this knowledge and eventually escape from the landlord's estate for a more independent life in the larger towns.

The second clip to be discussed precedes this first flashback sequence, the Quirce flashback, and explains the young man's situation in the new time frame—that is, a year or so after the death of Iván. As the director's name appears at the end of the second pre-narrative segment (the family photograph), the sound of a machine is heard on the soundtrack. This noise, the motif of the dangling diegetic signifier, materializes in the next shot (the opening sequence of the film) into the image of an approaching train. Quirce will step off this train. The rapidly approaching train of the opening sequence is a highly coded sign. A classic phallic symbol, the large and powerful image represents the paradigmatic power of the patriarch as father (literally) and controller (politically) of both family and society. However, in context of the adaptation's step into the future, the train as signifier represents another ideologically-bound signified. For the novel, traditional patriarchal values suppress the landless peasants at the poverty level. The film recontextualizes the sense of power by locating the paradigm (the train) in a new spatio-temporal relation outside the confines of the estate and after Quirce has left the image of a powerful, rushing train equals a force for progress.

The train pulls into a town. A lettered sign reads "Zafra," the name of a real town in the province of Badajoz, Extremadura. The sign situates the action of the film in a province, which, for its part, is an indexical sign of a region (Extremadura) that historically connotes latifundia, landowners, and landless peasants. The few people on the platform and those boarding with suitcases suggest that emigration to the cities has taken a toll on this town. Several people, including a young priest, a group of young soldiers, and two women in black, stand out as signifiers. In effect, the opening scene says, "This is an index of Spain." The train is a sign of progress; the soldiers a sign of the military and therefore of Franco; the priest is sign of the ubiquitous presence of Catholicism; and the women in black are a sign of traditional Catholic values, in this case mourning. All of these signs are contextualized in the province of Extremadura, the land of absentee landowners. Yet the powerful image of the train, a symbol *par excellence* of progress for this traditionally poor and oppressed province, overwhelms the apparently negative connotations of the other images. The camaraderie among the soldiers, who shake hands and wave to each other, undermines the negativity associated with the military service. The young priest, rushing away from the camera toward the waiting train, suggests that his importance as an authority figure is also undermined. In addition, his youth (rolled up jeans visible under his cassock) is associated with that of the soldiers and with the vitality of the train. All three come to represent a new age for Spain.

179

One of the soldiers enters the station's bar. The young man, who soon proves to be Quirce, asks curtly for a coffee, "Un café"; he does not say "por favor" (please). The reader has learned from the novel, and the viewer will see in the cinematic text, that Quirce's demeanor is consistently taciturn. He carefully takes out a notebook and pen. A close-up shot allows the viewer to see that he is indeed young, despite his mustache, and that he has a rather sweet face. This further characterizes the novel's representation of Quirce, who, despite his silence and surliness, plays sad tunes on his harmonica in the evenings. Quirce first thinks, then carefully writes "Hermana Nieves" (Sister Nieves). The camera then cuts to a young woman working in a modern factory and wearing a spotlessly clean uniform. The film has moved quickly through time and space to connect Quirce with Nieves, who also has left the estate and apparently works in or near Zafra. We see her receiving and then reading her brother's letter and realize that she also has learned how to read and write. Her presence reinforces the sense of futurity taking shape in this opening sequence.

Los santos inocentes is an example of a cinematic adaptation attempting to re-present the structure and tone of the written text. At the same time, the film intentionally deviates from the static temporal plane of the novel to create its own more positive level of meaning. While all adaptations vary greatly in the degree to which they approximate and deviate from the original text, the student and teacher of literature may use a cinematic adaptation to locate intersections and variants of both texts. He or she will ask the questions why, how, to what purpose, and with what result does each text create meaning. These questions are new tools with which to analyze the two media, and their answers will provide refreshing insights into the workings of both literary and cinematic texts.

Bibliography

Dudley Andrew, *Concepts in Film Theory* (Oxford: Oxford University Press, 1984).

Dudley Andrew, *The Major Film Theories: An Introduction* (London: Oxford University Press, 1976).

Jonathan Culler, *Structural Poetics: Structuralism, Linguistics, and the Study of Literature*

Miguel Delibes, *Los santos inocentes 1981.* (Barcelona: Editorial Planeta, 1982).

Terry Eagleton, *Literary Theory: An Introduction 1983.* (Minneapolis: University of Minnesota Press, 1985).

Wolfgang Iser, *The Act of Reading: A Theory of Aesthetic Response, 1976.* Trans. Der Akt des Lesens. (Baltimore: The Johns Hopkins University Press, 1980).

INDEX